HARVARD STUDIES IN ENGLISH

WORDSWORTH'S ANTI-CLIMAX

BY

WILLARD L. SPERRY

WORDSWORTH'S
ANTI-CLIMAX

BY

WILLARD L. SPERRY

NEW YORK / RUSSELL & RUSSELL

1966

PREFACE

PROFESSOR GARROD says that the last forty years of Wordsworth's life are "the most dismal anti-climax of which the history of literature holds record."[1]

When we have made due allowance for overstatement, these words serve for substance of doctrine. Coleridge, Crabb Robinson, and other wise friends were aware that the verse of the poet's latter years was not as good as that which had preceded it. Meanwhile it had taken Wordsworth thirty years to create the taste by which he could be appreciated, and when recognition came in the 1830's his converts were so undiscriminating that they imputed to the poetry he was then writing the virtues which they had discovered in the work of the first and greatest period of his literary history.

At this distance, however, there are few persons who habitually reread any considerable passages written later than *The Excursion*. We no longer assume that a poem must be good because Wordsworth wrote it. Indeed, our assumption is that, unless it antedates 1806–08, it is likely to be poor. Attempts have been made to rehabilitate "the later Wordsworth," but they tax the ingenuity of their authors and the credulity of their public.

The work of the poet's last thirty or forty years can be praised only at the expense of that of the eight or ten years after 1797. We cannot have it both ways. We do best therefore to trust the instinct which inclines us to the earlier work. It is a pity that the anti-climax came so soon and lasted so long, just as it is a pity that the southern end of the Lake District is not as lovely as the northern. Read-

1. H. W. Garrod, *Wordsworth* (Oxford: Clarendon Press, 1923), p. 138.

ing Wordsworth chronologically is much like tramping
from Keswick to Ambleside; the wildest and most beautiful scenery comes first, that which follows is by comparison
tame and even insipid.

On the other hand, we have not solved a problem in admitting Wordsworth's anti-climax; we have stated one.
Its nature is baffling, and its causes are obscure. I propose
in this book to reexamine the various answers which have
been given to the riddle. No single solution is convincing,
since each is made plausible only by ignoring stubborn
facts which point in other directions. William Wordsworth is proving to be an elusive person. He refuses to be
neatly dissected and disposed of in the critical laboratory.
Meanwhile, the more clearly we understand the causes of
his rise and fall as an artist, the deeper will be our insight
into his best work.

In the first two chapters of the book I have indicated
the setting of the critical stage, and have pointed out the
kind of action which takes place upon it.

In the following five chapters I have examined the reasons usually alleged for Wordsworth's poetic decline: his
premature old age, his break with Coleridge, his defection
from republicanism, his profession of Toryism and Anglicanism, his affair with Annette Vallon, and the hostile
criticism for which Francis Jeffrey was the spokesman.
The chapters take us over all the contested ground in recent criticisms of Wordsworth. Since none of these causes
seems to me adequate to account for the effect, I have advanced in the eighth chapter some further reflections on
the problem. I am persuaded that the answer to the riddle
of Wordsworth's anti-climax lies somewhere within the
area which in this chapter I have tried to define.

The concluding pages of the book deal with Wordsworth's major ideas, as they were the yield of his experience. His personal history did not coincide at all points
with his professional misadventure. That misadventure

seems to have been the sort of technical accident which might befall any poet. Therefore his treatment of nature, religion, and ethics deserves independent consideration.

I have made free use of much of the criticism of Wordsworth by his contemporaries, and I have quoted constantly from the familiar sources — the journals, the letters, and the prose works. I have not thought it necessary in each instance to give the reference. If a quotation brings us on controversial ground I have indicated the source. Otherwise, good faith and good conscience do not seem to require a regiment of footnotes to vindicate familiarity with sources which have become, by this time, the common property of those who write about Wordsworth. Quotations from *The Prelude* are taken from Mr. de Selincourt's edition of the 1805 text.

I wish to thank two friends, Professor A. W. Vernon and Professor J. B. Munn, for reading my manuscript while it was still in process and for making many valuable suggestions.

W. L. SPERRY

CAMBRIDGE, MASSACHUSETTS
October 19, 1934

CONTENTS

I

THE PRACTICE OF POETRY

II

THE CONDUCT OF LIFE

I

THE PRACTICE OF POETRY

CHAPTER I

Changing Perspectives

IN 1880 a group of persons — we might even say "personages" — met at Grasmere to organize the Wordsworth Society. Could he have foreseen the gathering, Francis Jeffrey would have been disconcerted. He had refused, at the beginning of the century, to introduce Wordsworth to the "intelligent and affectionate men in the upper ranks of society" who subscribed to *The Edinburgh Review*, and had relegated him to the company of "sentimental savages and preaching pedlars." But here were persons of Jeffrey's own kind met to honor a poet whom he had done his best to discredit — Matthew Arnold, Hutton of *The Spectator*, J. H. Shorthouse, Stopford Brooke, Aubrey de Vere, the Honorable Roden Noel, James Bryce, Lord Selbourne, Lord Houghton. It was as though Lord Jeffrey's drawing-room had adjourned to the Lake District.

The published proceedings of the Wordsworth Society mark a lull between two storms. For the first twenty or thirty years of his productive life Wordsworth had been the center of a spirited controversy. And now again, in our time, he has become the disputed subject of a divided criticism. For this reason the 1880's furnish a quiet spot from which to review

> old, unhappy far-off things,
> And battles long ago,

and to anticipate the revival of the dispute in those new terms which mark the more recent studies in the field.

The Society aimed to gather, while there were persons still living who remembered the poet, such intimate facts as had escaped the coarse meshes of Christopher Wordsworth's biography, to issue an accurate bibliography of the many editions of the poems (there were thirty-three of them from 1793 to 1850), and to put in definitive form a critical appraisal of the entire *corpus*. Pursuant to these ends, the papers read at the annual meetings were compounded of interesting local gossip, which even at that late date could be had for the asking in the Lake District, of excerpts from unpublished journals and letters, and of formal pronouncements upon the poet's contribution to letters, philosophy, statecraft, and religion.

George Tyrrell used to say that no religious society should outlast the second generation of the founder's disciples. With their passing the society should disband to save the spirit of the master from the letter of the institution. The Wordsworth Society seems to have held a similar view of itself, its hero, and its mission. It pursued its methodical way for six years and was then dissolved. In his last annual report the Honorary Secretary presented a letter from the Honorary Treasurer which voiced the motives that had prompted both the forming and the ending of the society:

I should like to protest against the needless disclaimers of being "Wordsworthians," which we have heard and read from some of the distinguished members of the Society — Mr. Ruskin, Mr. Arnold, Mr. Lowell, Professor Nichol and others. If a man has never been a "Wordsworthian" it is his misfortune, if not also his fault. On no other condition can the power of Wordsworth be fully realised; and most of us who were Wordsworthians once, but are so no longer, have probably less to regret or be ashamed of in what we were than in what we have become. . . . The question is not, Have you perceived the limitations? but, Have you received the inspiration? . . . Having once been a Wordsworthian, a man always remains a possible one. The world is too much with most of us; but "in seasons of calm weather," the old inspiration revives. . . . We become Wordsworthians again.[1]

This is the evangelical faith. Anyone who is familiar with the literature of sectarian movements can recognize the voice of the second generation of disciples. The early enthusiasm is still a remembered experience, but the moral mystery of the lapsed believer has begun to make its appearance. The defection is not active disbelief; rather, it is the listless consent, more deadly than doubt, which we give to a platitude. Matthew Arnold describes us, in such a state, as "light hearted believers of our casual creeds." Coleridge explains the casualness:

Truths, of all others the most awful and interesting, are too often considered as so true, that they lose all power of truth, and lie bed-ridden in the dormitory of the soul, side by side with the most despised and exploded errors.[2]

If the proceedings of the Wordsworth Society are an index of critical opinion in the 1880's, they suggest that the truth of Wordsworth was in danger of lapsing to the level of platitude. To save the poet and themselves, if not the rest of the world, from a living death, the members of the Society by common consent dissolved their organization in 1886. "It is much better," said the Honorary Chairman of the final meeting, "that the Society should end when there is perfect reality about it, than that anything connected with Wordsworth should degenerate into a mere name." The fragments had all been gathered up, and so far as they knew nothing had been lost.

The air of finality which surrounds the Society's transactions inspired James Russell Lowell's presidential address at the annual meeting of 1884. "Whatever can be profit-

1. *Transactions of the Wordsworth Society*, No. 8 (meeting of 1886), p. iv.
2. Samuel Taylor Coleridge, *Aids to Reflection* (New York: N. Tibbals and Son, 1872), p. 1.

ably said of him has already been said, what is said for the mere sake of saying it is not worth saying at all." Despite this preamble, which would seem to forbid further remarks on the subject, Mr. Lowell, after the manner of presiding officers, went on to make a long speech. But his words sound like falling clods on the coffin lid. He and his fellow Wordsworthians were committing the dust of the poet's more prosy numbers to its dust, and rendering up the spirit of the deathless verse to the muse that gave it. From first to last the proceedings imply that further criticism will be redundant, and that only curious ghouls will disturb thereafter the literary remains of William Wordsworth. Such was the state of the poet's fame during the last decades of the nineteenth century. In the face of the stupid and malignant criticism with which his early work had been greeted, Wordsworth had finally created a taste by which he could be appreciated. The suggestion of egotism, which had attended his youthful prophecies of literary immortality, had lost its arrogance by 1880, and we have in retrospect an almost Messianic self-confidence, fully warranted by the eventuality.

The road had had many turnings since 1798. For the first thirty years of his productive life Wordsworth had been in opposition. From about 1830 his reputation was in the ascendant, and by 1840 he had become a convention. But precisely to the degree that he had ceased to be a center of controversy and had become an idol, accurate insight into his work had waned. He was at the nadir of his literary influence at the time of his death in 1850.

The next twenty years added nothing to Wordsworth's reputation or to a better understanding of his work. The 1870's, however, gave us three brief studies of the first importance. The earliest was an article in *Macmillan's Magazine* (1873), by Sir John Duke Coleridge, which reawakened men's minds to a Wordsworth who was almost forgotten: "he is not generally appreciated, even now he is far too little read." The second was Leslie Stephen's penetrating analysis, *Wordsworth's Ethics* (1876), and the third was Matthew Arnold's famous essay (1879), which still remains the most authoritative pronouncement upon the poet for the half century after his death. The initial effect of this later criticism was to remove Wordsworth from the risk of further vilification, and to set him in a place of calm and honor. Nevertheless, the essays of the time, in so far as they were works of praise rather than of blame, acted as an opiate on the public mind. Wordsworth became over-respectable, and by the end of the century his verse was accepted as so true that it had lost its power of truth and had lapsed again into that half-alive state in which his death had overtaken him and all his affairs in 1850.

In 1896 Professor Emile Legouis published *La Jeunesse de William Wordsworth*. His book marks the beginning of the present period of Wordsworth criticism; one in which we are still involved and through which we are working our uncertain way. The date of Legouis' work was a happy accident, coming as it did so near the centenary of the *Lyrical Ballads*. It was natural and perhaps inevitable that a Frenchman should write this book.

Lowell had told the Wordsworth Society in 1884 that what is said about Wordsworth for the mere sake of saying it is not worth saying. No one disputes the truism, which obtains for all words on all subjects. But Lowell's major premise is open to question — the Olympian statement that everything which could profitably be said about Wordsworth had by that time been said.

There is in Horne's *New Spirit of the Age* (1844) a chapter devoted in part to Wordsworth. The author is saying that Wordsworth came upon the scene after a long decline of English poetry:

Looking back to the experience of nations, a national literature is seldom observed to recover its voice after an absolute declension; the scattered gleaners may be singing in the stubble, but the great song of the harvest sounds but once. . . . [Yet] England did not wait in vain for a new effluence of genius — it came at last like the morning — a pale light in the sky, an awakening bird, and a sunburst — we had Cowper — we had Burns — that lark of the new grey dawn; and presently the early risers of the land could see to spell slowly out the name of William Wordsworth.

James Russell Lowell expected after his time a waning insight into Wordsworth. There might be, there probably would be, random singing in the stubble; men saying things for the mere sake of saying them. But the great harvest hymn of the critical reaping was that being sung by himself and the men of his generation. Lowell was wrong, and his contemporaries fall, in varying degree, under like condemnation.

The defect of all Wordsworth criticism during the last half of the nineteenth century was its failure to take *The Prelude* seriously and to see in it an introduction to the poems of the great years. Today that obtuseness is hard to understand and even harder to condone. An early criticism of *The Prelude* says that in this, as in the rest of Wordsworth's verse, we read the record of "the author's uneventful and contemplative life." It is impossible to believe that the reviewer ever read the ninth and succeeding books; we can only say that, if he read them, his canons for eventful living excite our respect!

The difficulty was that the stormy later books of this work gave the lie to the effigy already in place. It was too much trouble to remove the effigy and to substitute the man. *The Prelude* was greeted with incredulity and dismissed with a studied indifference. As autobiography it was described as "a large fossil relic," and its final books, dealing with the French Revolution, seemed "strange pieces of furniture to be found in the soul of a laureate." If the readers of 1850 felt any discrepancy between the youthful hero of this metrical tale and the traditional Wordsworth upon whom they were by that time agreed, so much the worse for the hero. He was a late pretender who could not unthrone the effigy.

Matthew Arnold seems much to blame for having failed to correct the tradition by the truth, yet there was warrant for his handling of the subject. Leslie Stephen had already written his tract on *Wordsworth's Ethics*, and, since his name is mentioned in Arnold's essay, we may assume that he was its occasion. Meanwhile Leslie Stephen had been much nearer the truth than he could have realized. He saw that at some time in his life Wordsworth had been through a hard experience, and that the correction of the consequent despondency had been costly. He found the clue to Wordsworth's verse in a private history, veiled rather than revealed in the verse. Stephen thus anticipated the critics of our day in appealing from the poems to the personal experience which had occasioned them. Such treatment seemed to Arnold to put Stephen among the Wordsworthians and to sanction a type of literary criticism which he deplored and proposed to combat.

The 1879 essay was intended as a candid rebuke of Leslie Stephen and a frontal attack on those who still insisted on subordinating Wordsworth the poet to Wordsworth the man. Since *The Prelude* did not suit Matthew Arnold's uses, he left it to one side. The person whom Arnold would vindicate was the poet of nature and of homely human lives lived near to nature, a revealer of the tranquil English scene which, with rare exceptions, had been so long unnoticed and unsung. It was not the office of Arnold's Wordsworth to involve us in political revolutions or in psychological crises; rather,

> He laid us as we lay at birth
> On the cool flowery lap of earth.

Matthew Arnold was no stranger to melancholy, or to despondency needing correction, but he never made his peace with the darker side of life. He refused, therefore, to reckon in Wordsworth with facts which he preferred to ignore in himself. Against such unwelcome second thoughts his classical humanism was a laboriously constructed defense. There was in Arnold something of the romanticist, with the liability to suffering in which romanticism involves us, never acknowledged and to the end unresolved. Had he chosen to do so, he might have understood what Leslie Stephen had said about Wordsworth and thus might have conceded the Wordsworth of whom Stephen had spoken with uncanny insight; he chose not to do so.

We must remember also that, to the members of an Oxford upper common-room in the third quarter of the century, the French Revolution was no longer a contemporary event. There were few men then living to whom it was a poignant memory from early youth. Yet it had not slipped into that middle distance whence it could be recovered by historical research. England, after her immemorial manner, had put behind her the whole difficult time from the Terror through Waterloo and had passed on to other things.

Even had Arnold gone out of his way to make a place for the young and revolutionary Wordsworth, that phase of the poet's history was not one with which he and his fellows were concerned. As men of letters they were interested in the Wordsworth who had written *Michael*, and Arnold saw quite truly that this was the authentic Wordsworth. He did not see, or he refused to see, that Wordsworth, the author of *Michael*, could never have come to pass in want of the Wordsworth whom Leslie Stephen had identified. Both men were right; Arnold in insisting upon the pure poetry of Wordsworth in neglect of the system-monger, Stephen in realizing that the system could not be eradicated from a poetry which it had occasioned. But such was the weight of Arnold's influence that he suppressed for another twenty years all attempts to penetrate the secret of Wordsworth's elusive system, and allowed us only the poetry for the poetry's sake. Hence, at the time when mature critical judgments of Wordsworth were crystallizing, a great deal of relevant material was ignored. In spite of James Russell Lowell, it remained true that, at any time during the latter half of the nineteenth century, there was much which could profitably have been said about Wordsworth and which went unsaid. It is Professor Legouis' distinction as a critic to have said, in his study of Wordsworth's youth, what English critics of the previous half century had been either unable or unwilling to say.

There are some men, as Browning has it, who being born too soon are laid away in a great trance, the years coming and going all the while, until their true time's advent. In certain respects William Wordsworth was such a man. Given Cowper and Gray, it may be false to say that he was born out of due time and that he is unintelligible in the terms of his own day. Hazlitt, indeed, held that Wordsworth's genius was "a pure emanation of the spirit of the age." Meanwhile the metaphor of the trance is faithful to Wordsworth's reputation for fifty years after he had been acknowledged. The poet himself unhappily passed into trance some years before his death — being self-deceived about the excellence of his later verse. From about 1835 his work lived on in a state of suspended vitality. With the turning of the century Legouis broke the spell. He roused the poet from his sleep of conventional respectability and made him walk the ways of the world as a passionate youth, a rebel soul.

Ten or fifteen years later, Professor Harper enlisted Professor Legouis' help in discovering the truth of the affair with Annette. That story, long concealed, shattered the effigy beyond repair and ended a devout but unwarranted idolatry. Annette has confirmed the impressions given us in Legouis' first work and at the same time has complicated its issues. Matthew Arnold would have dis-

missed her as a preposterous hussy, but, with our greater
interest in the poet's youth and our better knowledge of it,
she has not put the Wordsworth whom we now know out
of character. Annette today is neither improbable nor incredible; indeed in retrospect she is seen to be necessary to
the interpretation of certain poems which fail to explain
themselves and which, on Matthew Arnold's premise, are
obscure if not inexplicable.

Our age returns with fresh interest to Wordsworth because we discover in him one who lived through a time not
unlike our own. He was no stranger to the idealism, the
disillusionment, and the cynicism of a generation which
has passed through a great war. Our extremity, matching
his distress, makes him a friend of the modern mind. We
are fitted, by virtue of our circumstance, to understand
him as the men of the serene 1880's could not understand
him. Yet, having said so much, one hears the voice of
Matthew Arnold calling us back from all ulterior considerations to the safe fold of the poetry for the poetry's sake.
We can even hear Wordsworth himself insisting that a
poet shall be judged by his work rather than by his life.
Such is the integrity of the moral order that we can vindicate an interested reading of Wordsworth only by a prior
disinterested reading. The critical issues stand in their
own right and must be dealt with on their own merits before we attempt to estimate their meaning and profit to us
for modern times. We must keep at arm's length the constant temptation to equate Wordsworth's life and work in
the terms of the twentieth century. He was a man of the
eighteenth and early nineteenth centuries, and he must be
understood in the light of his own day.

Recent studies of Wordsworth should satisfy us that we
have not now, and probably never shall have, facts in sufficient number and of adequate nature to give us an understanding of the man and his work upon which we may all
be agreed. William Ernest Henley said of him that he was

"a kind of inspired clergyman." For fifty years after his
death most of his readers subscribed to some such account
of the poet's nature and character. That unanimity is
gone. Today we are disagreed about Wordsworth, and
our disagreement gives us the intellectual pleasure which
arises from "the perception of dissimilitude in similitude,"
a principle which the poet himself had invoked in explanation of his art.

It has been said of another biographical study, "Such is
the character of the problem that historical experiment
must take the place of historical research. . . . Each individual creates him in accordance with his own character." [1]
A similar premise determines the criticism of Wordsworth.
Such facts as we have do not tell a forthright story. Hence
we must submit a critical hypothesis to the sources in an
attempt to interpret them. In so doing we impute our own
experience to the man whose life and work we would understand. Only at the expense of such a risk can biography,
as distinct from chronicle, be written. Therefore, given
the equivocal nature of the sources, we write a measure of
autobiography unwittingly, if not wittingly, when we pro-
nounce on Wordsworth.

Professor Garrod puts our present dilemma in a single
picturesque metaphor when he says that instead of the
"Daddy Wordsworth" of the last century (the term was
Fitzgerald's), we now have a "Byronic Wordsworth." [2]
Up to a point the latter figure is the creature of our own
tempers. He is the routine product of the biography of
detraction recently in fashion. The change conforms to the
altered manners of the age. Yet when all necessary allowance has been made for a Wordsworth who can be the idol
of the immoralists of the twentieth century, there is a
stubborn residuum of original fact which requires, if not

1. Albert Schweitzer, *The Quest of the Historical Jesus* (London: Adam and
Charles Black, 1911), pp. 4, 9.
2. H. W. Garrod, *Wordsworth* (Oxford: Clarendon Press, 1923), pp. 21–22.

the Byronic Wordsworth, at least some figure quite other than that which was venerated in Victorian times. (Differences of taste and morals to one side, a fresh estimate of Wordsworth as a man and a poet is inevitable.

At the moment the man is faring badly at the hands of the critics, and in consequence the good name of his poetry is suffering. If the present fashion is to prevail, Wordsworth will be unseated from the place which Arnold assigned him, second in English letters only to Shakespeare and Milton, and will become a neglected author because a discredited character. His work will be used as clinical material by those who are concerned with moral pathology, but it will have lost its healing power.

Given a Byronic Wordsworth in place of Daddy Wordsworth, which of the two was the true man? If both were in some measure true, how was the former metamorphosed into the latter? If such a change took place did it cost the man his integrity of character and the poet his excellence as an artist? The change, in some form or other, is conceded. Its causes and its nature are obscure. As the result of the last thirty or forty years of intensive study of Wordsworth a half-dozen stubborn problems still persist. The statement of the problems and proffered answers to them are the substance of this book. We shall understand and appraise at its true meaning Wordsworth's anti-climax only as we are successful in reading these specific riddles.

CHAPTER II

On the Reading of Wordsworth

WORDSWORTH wrote poetry for fifty years. Had he been jealous for his reputation he would have shortened the period to twenty years. By 1820 reviewers were already hinting that as a poet he had "lived too long," had "touched upon superannuation." Even Crabb Robinson, with the completed works finally before him, could not deny the unpalatable fact: "When I look at the single volume which comprehends the whole collection, I feel some apprehension that any young person who may open it will be inclined to shut it again, and look no further than the title."

From a very early time the remedy was obvious — an anthology. Indeed, Walter Pater has said that of all poets equally great Wordsworth profits most by an anthology. The matter had been mooted early. In 1819 we find *The Eclectic Review* saying:

Mr. Wordsworth has one chance of being read by posterity. It rests upon his finding some judicious friend to do for him the kind office which Pope did for Parnell, and which has probably saved his fame. If Wordsworth's best pieces could be collected into one volume, some of his early lyrics, a few of his odes, his noble sonnets, all his landscape sketches and the best part of the Excursion, while his idiots and waggoners were collected into a bonfire on the top of Skiddaw, the "Sybilline leaves" would form a most precious addition to our literature.

Two or three years later the poet conceded the probability of some such volume, though it must have gone against the grain to allow the distinction between a better and a worse, to say nothing of a good and a bad. Nevertheless, "the selection you again advert to will no doubt be executed at some future time." Hine's *Selections from the Poems of William Wordsworth* appeared with the author's sanction in 1831. The poet thought "the collection judiciously made." Ten years later Aubrey de Vere was interesting himself in a second similar volume. The classical anthologies have come later, particularly Arnold's, and have been so deservedly successful that Sir Walter Raleigh has now said,

The finest part of his work has been separated from the inferior bulk, so that new readers of his poetry may make straight for the noblest numbers, without wasting time in reading what the poet, less happy than they, wasted time in writing. Is there anything worth doing, it may be asked, that yet remains to be done? [1]

This is the question which James Russell Lowell had asked the Wordsworth Society forty years earlier and had answered in the negative.

Were Pater and Arnold right, the one in theory and the other in practice? May it not be that of all poets equally great Wordsworth is most mutilated and most misrepresented by an anthology? The case is justiciable. During his lifetime Wordsworth decreed that, if there were to be anthologies, they should not omit the poems which had given most offense. He regarded these as the test cases. So far from allowing them to be burnt on the top of Skiddaw, he insisted that they should be given places of Olympian honor with the noblest numbers. His critics found him inflexible and conceded the point. A writer in *Frazer's Magazine* (1832) says:

1. Walter Raleigh, *Wordsworth* (London: Edward Arnold and Company, 1925), p. 2.

Any man of common sense in half an hour would, by blotting out a couple of dozen pages from Wordsworth's works, render them secure from criticism; but those very couple of dozen are the pages which he would most strenuously insist on retaining, stunning you with oratory to prove them the most superb things ever composed.

In the Wordsworth universe there should be no intimations of immortality denied his idiots and tinkers. While he was still alive and master of his literary fortunes the poet stubbornly reprinted the disputed verses in each new edition. Since his death anthologists have followed his precedent, not because the poems themselves uniformly merit further life, but because they are historic battlefields of English letters.

As for the less controverted pieces, there never has been exact agreement about their number and their limits. Sir Walter Raleigh is hardly justified in saying that the best poems have all been lifted from the inferior bulk. Wordsworth foresaw the difficulty from the first. He wrote to Moxon in 1831, "you would find no two persons agreeing upon what was best." As usual he knew his own work better than the critics knew it.

The present tendency is to increase rather than to decrease the bulk of the Wordsworth anthology. Poems formerly omitted are now being given preferment. In particular the latest anthologies do not dismiss as insoluble the editorial difficulty presented by *The Prelude* and *The Excursion*.[1] Modern compilers, by including parts of these works, imply that they are not, and perhaps were never intended to be, poems in their entirety. *The Prelude* in particular is a long discussion, both autobiographical and analytical, of the mental processes out of which poetry comes, together with much relevant and irrelevant reference to political events of the day. The

1. Cf. *Selected Poems of William Wordsworth* (Oxford University Press, Humphrey Milford, 1913).

analysis of the working of a poet's mind is from time to time punctuated by short poems intended to illustrate and to vindicate the psychology. *The Prelude* so construed becomes intelligible and readable.

In theory Wordsworth believed in his plenary verbal inspiration. Yet his faith did not prevent him from seeing his poems in something like perspective. Many of his best verses were originally written as short, self-contained pieces, which were inserted later into longer and more labored works. He did not find such a method of composition satisfactory. He tells a friend, "To write fragments of verse is an embarrassing practice," since one is tempted, when busy with a more ambitious work, "to lug on these ready-made pieces by the head and shoulders." [1] That is what happened to the lines about rowing and skating finally lodged in the first book of *The Prelude*. Apparently Wordsworth himself was aware of the resulting ambiguity, but, even if he was not, his earliest critics were. Henry Taylor, writing in *The Quarterly Review*, says that *The Excursion* cannot be read in its entirety as a poem; in a poem on so large a scale much must be prosaic. If it were all of uniform intensity we could not read more than ten pages at a time — and the quarto original ran to hundreds of pages! An artist of Wordsworth's ability

will know that it behooves him to apply himself from time to time to manage his own transitions, and *transact* the *business* of his poem. . . . Mr. Wordsworth, in his great work, copiously poetical as he is, uses his stores with a measured plenty, after the manner of a captain of a ship bound upon a long voyage, who, if he has no fears for the exhaustion of his resources, must yet look to the wholesome feeding of his crew, well knowing that their "alacrity and cheer of mind" depends upon it, and that it were better their diet should be occasionally dry as "the remainder biscuit," than that they should be heated and gorged.

---

1. W. W. to R. P. Gillies, December 22, 1814.

The latest editorial practice in the making of a Wordsworth anthology follows this hint of a century ago, and in
so doing is more faithful to the poet's total work than were
the earlier volumes of selections. The present custom of
including short passages from *The Prelude* and *The Excursion* has rendered the protracted poems to some degree
accessible to the new reader. Through the breach thus
made even the layman is let into these forbidding, if not
forbidden, cities.

Meanwhile, why do we read Wordsworth at all? He is
hard reading, and there are dreary stretches of him which
are wholly unrewarding, so far as any immediate pleasure
is concerned. To the credit of his contemporaries it should
be said that certain of them were quite aware of the heavy
demand which Wordsworth makes on his reader. *The
Dublin University Magazine* (1835) tells us that

in Wordsworth's poetry, — in every line of it — his reader is
forced to think. . . . To him who does not think and examine
his own thoughts — who cannot be alone with his own heart, in
the calmness of that self-communion, which excludes everything
that arises to intercept and conceal him from himself, Wordsworth must be for the greater part unintelligible. If to be the
instrument of creating anew in the heart its past feelings be, in
truth, what was meant by those who, in the meditative times of
old, gave to the poets their name of *poet* or *creator*, never did uninspired writer make more severe demands on the exercise of
searching thought than has been done by Wordsworth.

Thus early critics began to see that "Mr. Wordsworth
never intended so to write that those who ran might read";
he must be "read studiously."

The answer to our question is intimated in a penetrating
comment made by a reviewer just a hundred years ago:
"Without him a grey cloak seen in the distance on a lonely
moor would have no meaning." [1] The sentence has some-

1. *The New Monthly Magazine*, 1835, part II, 12.

thing of the quality of Wordsworth's own best verse; a
bareness, an austerity, a restraint, and a strong suggestion
of solitude. Each word has been weighed with care to its
fitness, and all the words together achieve the strict economy of idea and the overflow of powerful feeling which
mark the authentic Wordsworth poem.

At a later time Arnold took his stand upon precisely this
ground. With unerring insight into the nature of Wordsworth's genius he picked out, as the one most characteristic line, the words from *Michael*,

> And never lifted up a single stone.

An old shepherd sitting motionless by an unfinished sheep-
fold, a gray cloak seen in the distance on a lonely moor, —
these are the Wordsworth whom we first knew and to
whom we always return. So far as we have any record, the
poet was only once treasonable to such scenes, when in a
youthful letter to William Matthews he voiced a moment's
impatience with the mountains and professed a preference
for Fleet Street.[1]

Wordsworth did not convert all his friends to Cumberland and Westmorland. Coleridge was a transient.
Southey used Keswick as a convenient base from which to
dream Oriental fictions. Wordsworth had the power to
rouse in Charles Lamb a passionate preference for the city.
And as for Francis Jeffrey, it was too much to ask or to
expect of him that he should unlearn at Wordsworth's feet
the gallantries of urbane life in Edinburgh. Not only so,
but in pointing to mountains and to the solitary human
figures descried on their sky-line, Wordsworth was opening
a source of beauty which was both unfamiliar and uncon-
genial to the rank of men. The eighteenth century had inherited the medieval dread of mountains, and in asking his
time to give the high hills a love which should cast out the
old fear — and Wordsworth wrote his best verse for men

1. W. W. to W. M., November 7, 1794.

of the eighteenth rather than of the nineteenth century —
he asked more than the common man could achieve.[1]

As for his human subjects, there had been Cowper and
Gray and Crabbe; therefore he was not an innovator. Yet,
in spite of these pioneers, it was Wordsworth who finally
domesticated plain people in the accepted letters of the
nineteenth century. If, at a much later time, Thomas
Hardy found it possible to write the Wessex novels without
explanatory prefaces, and Synge made Irish peasants speak
for themselves, they derived this power in no small part
from rights conferred upon them by Wordsworth. The
bare ground and red earth and men and women near the
soil, which are today among the most moving subjects
for verse and fiction, have become accessible through the
breach that Wordsworth made in the city-mindedness of
the late eighteenth century.

Perhaps this is all of Wordsworth; certainly it is the most
and the best, and may well be enough. When Matthew
Arnold identified and isolated this distinguishing excellence in Wordsworth, he served the poet well. If Wordsworth is allowed to fall into the hands of persons who prefer abstract systems to concrete images, he is betrayed.
Arnold was right in trying to put the ark of the covenanted
verse in some safe place where the philistines could not get
at it. As for Wordsworth's systems, there is not one of
them — esthetic, moral, or political — which is not second-
hand as we find it in his poetry and which may not be had
better in the prose original from which he took it. If we
wish the eighteenth-century doctrine of the association of
ideas, we should go to Hartley and Alison rather than to
The Prelude. Of all the systems which Wordsworth ex-
pounded in meter, the one most nearly the yield of his own
experience is his doctrine of "despondency corrected"

1. *A Description of the Scenery of the Lakes in the North of England*, 1822.
A Guide through the District of the Lakes in the North of England, 1835. *Kendal
and Windermere Railway*, 1844. In these prose works Wordsworth discusses
the popular dislike of mountain scenery.

upon which Leslie Stephen fastened. But even that theory is not original with Wordsworth, and as a matter of ethics is best studied in its classical exemplars. The more the pity that he found it necessary to do so much metrical system-mongering.

The difficulty is, however, that once we have read a poem like *Michael* we cannot suppress a desire to know how Wordsworth wrote it. The finished work is not self-explanatory. The meager idea and the restrained emotion are deceptive. The simplicity of any one of the best poems lies, not on the near side, but on the far side of a tedious and detailed discipline. The road thither is a *via negativa*, lined, as all such roads must be lined, by the renunciations it has required. Anyone who has ever tried to write the mother tongue knows that Wordsworth has worked, in *Michael*, a poem little short of a miracle. He had said that he proposed to revive the artless ballads of an earlier time and professed to have done so. But Wordsworth's affectation of artlessness does not conceal a complex history, a mature self-consciousness, even a sophistication which the old ballad lacked.

Contrary to common report Wordsworth is in many ways the least objective of the great English poets. He did not write about the order of the outer world; the human mind was the haunt and main region of his song, and he cited always the instance of the human mind which he knew best, his own mind. From first to last he never once suggested that his poetry was a direct transcript of gray cloaks and lonely moors; he gave us those facts as his acute sensibilities had recorded them and as his vivid imagination had recreated them. Although he aimed to write with his eye fixed steadily on his subject, he was aware that his vision was imputing to the subject a reality at once other and perhaps greater than that given in the actuality.

There are certain words or combinations of words which recur so constantly in Wordsworth's poetry as to be characteristic of him. Were we to find them wanting in any

given hundred lines of verse we should know that we
were not reading Wordsworth. One such hallmark is the
phrase "to me," and its variants, "for me," "by me,"
"with me," "in me." A kindred usage is that which com-
pounds words with "self" as a first member. "Self-
accused," "self-cherished," "self-contented," "self-de-
voted," "self-exiled," "self-glorified," "self-illumined,"
"self-reviewed," "self-stilled." Wordsworth can hardly
be credited with selflessness.[1]

Yet the use of pronouns in the first person was not conscious egotism with Wordsworth. It was not, at the first,
unconscious habit. It was a matter of nice distinction and
of good conscience, an insistence that in the making of any
work of art the mind must half create because it can only
half receive. The usage probably became second mental
nature with the years, even a convention at the last. But
in its initial form this subjective reference was Wordsworth's notice, served on the reader, that a poet does not
reproduce what he observes, he recreates it by an independent act of the imagination. Wordsworth's scrupulousness in calling attention to his method and the nature
of his work was an attempt to keep faith with the reader.

We must realize, then, that a poem so simple and de-
ceptively objective as *Michael* has its truest scene in the
poet's own mind. Not that Wordsworth was as pure a
subjectivist as Coleridge: he never held that Michael
lived only in his own mind; he merely insisted that a
transcript of sense experience could not tell the truth of
the old shepherd. A poet must be a man of preternatural
sensibility, but he must also be more than that.

A penetrating biography of a modern man of letters,
Notre Cher Péguy, yields this striking sentence, "Avec son
humour d'atelier, le vieux peintre Jean-Paul Laurens disait

1. "Conceit and egotism are the besetting sins of the school; the pronouns,
personal and possessive, *I*, *me*, *my*, *mine*, are put forward prominently on every
occasion." *The British and Foreign Review*, I (1835), 211. We must concede to
this ungenerous critic twenty-five poems beginning with the first personal pro-
noun.

en parlant de Péguy, 'Il nous fera toujours manger à la cuisine,' voulant signifier par là que sa prose donnait à la fois le repas et la préparation du repas." [1] Here is the characteristic note of modernity in letters. There was a similar quality in Wordsworth. Curiously enough a critic, writing in 1814, applies to the Lake Poets a quotation from the French very akin to Laurens' description of Péguy's prose method: "It is observed of Marivaux, by one of his countrymen, 'Il ne donne pas le résultat de son observation, mais l'acte même de l'observation.'" That is precisely what Wordsworth was forever trying to give us, not the result of observation, but the act itself. The endeavor was not then, and even with our more accurate psychology is not now, easy of fulfilment. Indeed, there is no type of writing more difficult, and it says much for Wordsworth that, with the imperfect apparatus which he had at hand for the attempt, he achieved such distinction.

By the end of his life Wordsworth had concluded that it was better not to let the general public behind the scenes where they might watch the stage management of the poetic act. He repented in particular of his prose prefaces, appendices, and essays-supplementary, and by 1830 he was blaming Coleridge for the publication of the critical apparatus. Coleridge was by that time equally unwilling to accept the responsibility for prefaces in which he no longer believed, and the letters of the two men leave them unfathered. The assumption is that Coleridge made the suggestion in the first instance and that Wordsworth put it into execution. Wordsworth's sober second thoughts convinced him that he had committed a strategic blunder:

The preface which I wrote long ago to my own poems I was persuaded to write by the urgent entreaties of a friend, and I

---

1. Jerome and Jean Tharaud, *Notre Cher Péguy* (Paris: Libraire Plon-Nourrit, 1926), II, 7.

heartily regret that I ever had anything to do with it; though I
do not reckon the principles then advanced erroneous.[1]

In the foregoing there is frequent reference to what is called
Mr. W's 'theory,' and his 'preface' to the *Lyrical Ballads*. I
will mention that I never cared a straw about the 'theory' and
the 'preface' was written at the request of Mr. Coleridge out of
sheer good nature. I can recollect the very spot . . . where he
pressed the thing upon me; and but for him it never would have
been thought of.[2]

Meanwhile the poems of the great period, even shorn of
the prose aids, are a veritable workshop. Wordsworth had
proposed a vast cathedral of verse, of which *The Recluse*
was to be the main body and the lesser poems "little cells,
oratories, and sepulchral recesses." This ambitious metaphor never commanded consent or caught the popular
fancy. A writer in *The Quarterly Review* refuses to be
impressed by the advertisement to *The Excursion*, failing
to find in "this conversation of four old gentlemen" any
likeness to a cathedral. A fellow-critic, willing to concede
the poet a tentative right to his figures of speech, remarks
with much truth that the result is more like "a large and
comfortless meeting-house than a cathedral!"[3] If we take
the poet at his own word, *The Recluse*, like many another
bold and unfinished work, must be called Wordsworth's
Folly. The cathedral stands incomplete. Meanwhile, in
so much of the work as was done, the processes of construction are still visible. Architect's plans, chisels, mal-
lets, half-cut and uncut stone are lying all about the site.
Much of the incidental scaffolding is still in place. So far
from visiting a finished and dedicated building we are let
into an area where the work is actually going on.

1. W. W. to John Abraham Heraud, November 23, 1830.
2. Note by W. W. penciled on the margin of a MS. by Barron Field.
3. Hazlitt in *The Spirit of the Age* changes Wordsworth's metaphor of a
cathedral to that of a dining-room and says that reading *The Excursion* is like
being ushered into a banquet-hall, seated with a company of clowns, and served
with successive courses of apple dumplings. "It was not even *toujours perdrix!*"

We have, thus, in Wordsworth's poetry, not merely the strong subjective element, — and in this Wordsworth was not peculiar, since all the poets of the time were unashamedly interested in themselves, — we have as well an interest in the technical making of poems creeping into the very act of creation, as though the process itself were the poetic end rather than a means. Hazlitt, whose judgments of Wordsworth became increasingly adverse, refers to this aspect of the poet's work as "an intense intellectual egotism." The phrase was barbed and touched with personal animus.

Other critics were more generous. Charles Lamb wrote to the poet soon after the appearance of the *Lyrical Ballads* of "the delicate and curious feeling in the wish for the 'Cumberland Beggar,' that he may have about him the melody of birds, although he hears them not. Here the mind knowingly passes a fiction upon herself, first substituting her own feeling for the 'Beggar' and in the same breath, detecting the fallacy, will not part with her wish." In 1844 a later critic presses the point still further: "It is more remarkable that he is what he is, not unconsciously or instinctively, but consciously, to all appearances, and determinately, and by a particular act of the will. Moreover he is not only a self-conscious thinker and feeler; but he is conscious, apparently, of this self-consciousness." [1]

Both of the passages are faithful to their occasion. The objective simplicity of a Wordsworth poem is deceptive. There is always an awareness of what is being thought and felt in the presence of the inciting subject, and an endeavor, which the reader is required to share, to catch the feelings and to record the ideas. It may be that Wordsworth was attempting the impossible, but, if so, his attempt is one which has been very generally renewed in our own time. Most modern writers are trying to overtake and to record

1. R. H. Horne, *A New Spirit of the Age* (New York: Harper and Brothers, 1844), p. 181.

themselves in the artistic act. The imagination itself rather than the objects upon which it is employed becomes thus the subject of the work. Whether or not Virginia Woolf and James Joyce and Marcel Proust succeed in the attempt may be an open question. But in so far as the type of literature they represent is characteristic of our time, Wordsworth was their forerunner, and a citizen of the twentieth century, rather than of the eighteenth and nineteenth centuries. His curious modernity must be one of the sources of the fresh interest in his work.[1] The objectification of self-consciousness and the esthetic transcript of the workings of the imagination may demand a mental subtlety beyond our human power. Obviously the intellectual involution required is a difficult act. But no one has come to the heart of Wordsworth's verse unless he is fully aware of the poet's quickened subjectivity in the presence of one or another of his chosen subjects from the outer world.

Pascal once said of our contact with a great book, "we look for an author and we find a man." That is precisely what happens to the reader of Wordsworth. The author, an impersonal maker of poetry, dissolves before us, and whether we will or no we are confronted by a man. There are few great poets in our tradition, perhaps none, whose essence so stubbornly refuses to be divided, and whose histories are so integral a part of their writing.

It does not avail that Wordsworth himself insisted upon the distinction between the poet and the private individual and deplored any confusion of the two persons. Not merely were his themes largely determined by his intimate history, but the introspective, subjective element in the work is so great, and the invitation to us to share in the

1. "Why is there suddenly so much interest in the human psyche as something to be experienced? This has not been the case for a thousand years." C. G. Jung, *Modern Man in Search of a Soul* (New York: Harcourt, Brace and Company, 1933), p. 34.

technical poetic act so compelling, that we cannot keep company with the poet alone, save as the poet be construed as the whole man.

The anthology can never do Wordsworth full justice and may do him a grave injustice. No anthology may delete poems concerned with the fortunes and operations of his mind. Every anthology includes *Tintern Abbey* and *The Daffodils*, and these poems — no more are necessary — are a breach in the dike sufficient to let in the whole flood of autobiographical concern. Once this material is conceded, none of it can be safely ignored. In the dreariest lines there are reaffirmations or restatements of poetic method, and even in the latest work there is an afterglow lighting up the earlier scene. Wordsworth remained so constant to the poetic faith he professed at the beginning of the golden decade — in so far as that faith dealt with the manner in which poems come to birth — that even on into the eighteen-forties we get shafts of insight falling back upon the nobler numbers, and helping us to understand them better.

> Dear native Regions, wheresoe'er shall close
> My mortal course, there will I think on you;
> Dying, will cast on you a backward look;
> Even as this setting sun . . .
> Doth with the fond remains of his last power
> Still linger, and a farewell lustre sheds
> On the dear mountain-tops where first he rose.[1]

We may not, therefore, define our Wordsworth too briefly or conclude him too soon. Hence we cannot safely hand over our final appreciation of him to an anthologist. We shall get much preliminary pleasure from a wise editor's harvesting, but we shall not have reaped the field. Once we have become interested in Wordsworth and involved with his work, the reading of his poetry is a matter of all or nothing.

1. This passage does not appear in the 1805 text of *The Prelude.*

CHAPTER III

The Decline

MATTHEW ARNOLD is to be credited with the now familiar phrase about Wordsworth's "golden decade," those years from 1798 to 1808 [1] in which "almost all his really first-rate work was done." The present critical fashion shortens this period by about two years and brings it to an end with the *Ode: Intimations of Immortality*, which was finished in 1806.

Like all dogmas, the theory that during his sixty years of literary life Wordsworth wrote first-rate poems for eight or ten years and third-rate verse for fifty years is over-simple. There are fine passages in *The Excursion* (1814), which may not be overlooked. There are noble lines, like those at the end of the *Duddon Sonnets* (1820), as authentic as any Wordsworth ever wrote. *The Memorials of a Tour in Italy* (1837) reaffirms, at times, his earlier power over words. As late as 1842 *To the Clouds* recovers something of the imperious mood of the great decade. Yet Wordsworth could not be relied upon, after about 1806, to write poetry which bore upon its face the credentials of its greatness, and, failing inspiration, he manufactured verses. In general, therefore, there is warrant for Professor Garrod's statement that the last forty years of Wordsworth's life are "the most dismal anti-climax of which the history of literature holds record."

This anti-climax, which was Wordsworth's point of

---

1. A more meticulous chronology would date this decade 1797-1807, since *Lyrical Ballads* was in process a year before its printing.

poetic arrival, has become our point of critical departure. We see the end from the beginning and read the early work in the light of the later. Much as we might like to isolate the poems of the golden decade and to rid ourselves of the embarrassment of the subsequent work, we cannot in good conscience do so. There must have been some initial defect which brought on untimely, and hastened unduly, the processes of Wordsworth's poetic decline. Hence we seek the sources of the last sterility in the nature of the first fruitfulness.

The fading of splendid visions is a commonplace of human experience. In the terms of his history as a poet Wordsworth brooded much over the riddle. His verse concedes that the glories which come to us in early life are a mystery in their advent and a reproach in their loss. He never ceases to ask why they are given only to be withdrawn, whether memory can recover them and imagination recreate them to give them a permanent life in the mind. He confined himself mainly to the literary problem, but was not able to rid himself of the suspicion that the technical perplexity had a deeper significance.

Perhaps the supposed problem of Wordsworth's decline is insoluble, simply because it is not a problem at all. Bad verse is not a riddle; any journeyman can write it. The riddle is good poetry. Where does it come from, how is it written, what conscious part has the author in its making? Are we not reversing the issues when we ask why Wordsworth wrote mediocre poems for forty years? The real question is, How was Wordsworth able to write good poems for eight or ten years?

Poets have usually said that their best work is the product of inspiration. They are from time to time visited by some creative power, not themselves, which fulfils their talent as genius. In this experience poets are like prophets, saints, mystics; and poetry is akin to religion. Indeed, for Wordsworth poetry and religion were so nearly identical

as to be indistinguishable.[1] Whether the faith common
to artists and mystics is warranted, because grounded in
the total reality of things, we do not know. We can only
say that the persons concerned have never been satisfied
with naturalistic accounts of the sources of their inspiration.

Wordsworth believed that he was a dedicated poet. He
was rather too solemn in speaking of his dedication, and he
is generally charged with undue egotism in the matter, but
it is hard to see how he could have given the world a faithful record of his inner history and yet have escaped the
charge. All men of genius have made the same claim and
have invited the same criticism. There is no known cir-
cumlocution by which a saint or an artist can avoid the
appearance of egotism. Infelicitous as Wordsworth may
have been in references to his vocation, any periphrasis
or false modesty would have been worse.

Meanwhile, no mystic has ever laid claim to constant
inspiration. The experience is occasional and fugitive, and
the classical literature of religious devotion is much concerned with the sorry anti-climaxes of the spiritual life.
The periods of inspiration seem to be few and brief; the
periods of dryness, bitterness, and of the dark night of the
soul, many and interminable. Uninspired days and years
stretch like a desert between rare oases of peace and power.
If we allow Wordsworth eight or ten years of inspiration
out of his sixty years of productive life, we can only say
that, as these matters go, the ratio is in his favor. Most
mystics have had to learn to be content with less. The
real problem would seem to be, why and how Wordsworth
maintained so high a level for so considerable a time as the
golden decade.

Nevertheless, there is in the arts, as in religion, a regimen which makes inspiration more likely than otherwise

1. See in his preface to the second edition of the *Lyrical Ballads* the passage
beginning, "What is a poet?"

it would be. "The poet, Wordsworth knew well," says
Ernest de Selincourt, "was a craftsman who must toil with
unremitting patience at every detail of his work, till it has
gained a clearer outline, a fuller substance; not otherwise
could it acquire that organic power which is the sure
touchstone of art." Although Wordsworth urged upon
others a wise passiveness, he was far from being a literary
quietist. In his finished work the apparatus for making
poetry is much in evidence. Only on the rarest occasions
does he succeed in deleting from his verse all traces of the
process of its composition. The *Tintern Abbey* lines are
Wordsworth at a very high level, yet they are concerned
with the manner of their own creation, and with the reassuring prospect of verses yet to come. There is something to be said for the theory that, working overmuch on
the often motionless machinery of his genius, Wordsworth
finally put it out of gear. I propose to return to this suggestion in a later chapter.

Within these general limits we have not merely a critical
right, we have a critical duty, to try to understand the connection between the golden decade and the sterile years
which followed. The inquiry now stands at the forefront
of all criticism of Wordsworth, and every question which
we ask about him turns out to be a facet of this major
problem. If we could understand the causes and the nature of Wordsworth's anti-climax as a poet, we should be
in a position to explain his worst verse, and, what is far
more important, to understand his best verse.

The task should be undertaken with a proper humility.
We belong to a generation which prides itself on its critical
acumen. We have no cause to preen ourselves because we
see clearly the prosiness of most of Wordsworth's later
work. The poet's more candid contemporaries were quite
aware that there was a falling-off. The journals and letters
of the time are filled with laments at the great man's iner-
tia. There was *The Prelude* gathering dust in its pigeon-

hole. Mrs. Wordsworth writes in wry humor from "Idle
Mount which just now well supports that title."

By about 1820 Coleridge was calling attention to the de-
clining excellence of Wordsworth's work. Crabb Robinson, than whom there was none more loyal, served notice
on his friend that better things might be expected. "A
poet who begins so early and so well as you did sets himself
a severe task in the implied obligation to maintain his
place." This was straight talk; we honor both its candor
and its courage. He writes even more frankly to Dorothy
and, having written, fears lest "the letter be thought impertinent"; yet he does not withdraw it, — he sends it,
half-fearing and half-hoping that it may be passed on to
the poet for his good. Plainly we have not allowed our
genius for criticism to create at this late date an adventitious difficulty on which to show our skill. The dismal fact
of the poet's waning powers was familiar to his immediate
circle.

Perhaps the true pathos of Wordsworth's decline is this,
that he could not disguise it from himself. The eleventh
book of *The Prelude* gives us the first intimation of a fear,
taking form in his mind, which was to mature in later
years into a somber certainty:

> the hiding-places of my power
> Seem open; I approach, and then they close;
> I see by glimpses now; when age comes on,
> May scarcely see at all.

Thereafter this note was never wholly silenced, and at
times it was the poet's dominant theme:

> Dread Power! whom peace and calmness serve
> No less than Nature's threatening voice,
> If aught unworthy be my choice,
> From THEE if I would swerve;
> Oh, let Thy grace remind me of the light
> Full early lost, and fruitlessly deplored;
> Which, at this moment, on my waking sight
> Appears to shine, by miracle restored;

My soul, though yet confined to earth,
Rejoices in a second birth!
— 'Tis past, the visionary splendor fades;
And night approaches with her shades.

He was forty-eight when he wrote the above lines, and there were more than thirty years to run. Wordsworth, with such passages to his credit, cannot be accused of immoderate self-assurance. He felt in his members the intimate poignancy of that anti-climax which is for us merely a literary perplexity.

In dealing with the dogma of the decline, as with the fact, we must remember that Wordsworth's time-sheet of years was not that which we expect the artist to keep. The lives of most poets have been fierce and brief; they have been written out and often dead by middle age. The days of Wordsworth's years were, by reason of strength, fourscore. Who knows what anti-climaxes we should have had to acknowledge and to regret had the productive lives of his contemporaries, Byron, Shelley, and Keats, reached to Wordsworth's great age? Death may well have been merciful to their literary names. They were all born after Wordsworth and died long before him. When we compare the shorter arc of their lives — Byron, 1788-1824; Shelley, 1792-1821; Keats, 1795-1821 — with that of Wordsworth, 1770-1850, we can understand that we are dealing here with facts which are incommensurable. He was born eighteen years before the earliest of this trio and outlived the last of them by twenty-six years. As for Coleridge, who was critic as well as creator, his life, 1772-1834, fell eighteen years short of Wordsworth's.

Of the great poets who worked in maturity at large canvasses we may say, with some measure of fidelity to fact, that their best verse was finished, or at least conceived and well under way, before they were fifty. Chaucer was forty-five when he finished *The Canterbury Tales*. Spenser published the first three books of *The Faerie Queene* in 1590, when he was thirty-eight. A second three followed in 1596. He was dead at forty-seven. Shakespeare's period of greatest productivity — the so-called "third period," which gave us *Hamlet, Othello, Macbeth,* and *Lear* among its ten or twelve plays — fell between the poet's thirty-sixth and forty-fifth years.. Both Dante and Milton worked to the end, and *The Divine Comedy* and *Paradise Lost* carried them into their fifties, but Dante had begun the former in his forties and Milton had conceived the latter in his late thirties.

Of the. moderns, Browning lived to something like Wordsworth's great age, but he wrote twenty years too long. The single volumes of Wordsworth and Browning, if printed in chronological order, divide at much the same place. We seldom go beyond *The Excursion* or *The Ring and the Book,* yet in each volume more than a third of the work is yet to come. The later Browning poems are marked by blemishes which even his greatest admirers cannot deny. But they cause us no resentment and create no literary problem; they are accepted as in the order of nature — the laborious work of an old man. If we judge Wordsworth otherwise, it is because we find in his earlier verse an austere excellence which Browning never achieved and to which, to do him justice, he never laid claim.

On any reasonable count, therefore, given the parallel of other literary lives, we may dismiss the last twenty, even the last thirty years, of Wordsworth's life as lying beyond the time when we have normal expectation of first-rate work from a poet. This takes us back to 1820. The period which compasses a culpable anti-climax is shortened to the ten or fifteen years which followed the golden decade. After 1820 on-coming age denied Wordsworth the power of sheer invention which is at its zenith in late youth and early manhood.[1]

1. I was once in a dinner group which included John Sargent. After-dinner talk centered about the fact that most of the English poets writing at the be-

Look at the other end of the calendar. Wordsworth was
late in his authentic arrival. Our modern interest in the
youthful Wordsworth concerns a time, when so far as his
art was concerned the poet was still in embryo. The
youthful Wordsworth was not writing poems; he was
idling, traveling, thinking, and feeling. Two or three short
poems follow his coming of age. In 1792-93 he wrote *Descriptive Sketches*. His two Godwinian ventures — *Guilt
and Sorrow* and *The Borderers*—fall between 1793 and 1796.
Descriptive Sketches, for all its promise, was in the elder
tradition; the Godwin poems were a passing phase and
throw light on a particular period of the poet's history;
neither belongs with his best work. Wordsworth's characteristic poetry began with the *Lyrical Ballads*. The authentic poet, who is deplored as a lost leader in his later
years, did not begin to write until he was nearly thirty.

We have, therefore, a Wordsworth finally embarked on
his first productive period at a time of life when, with the
average artist, the inventive power has begun to wane.
The pent-up energy burst out like a flood through a broken
dam. But in those first years of the golden decade Wordsworth was frankly experimenting both with his subjects
and with his medium at an age when most poets have decided upon the one and have mastered the other. Although
the initial energies of the artist may have begun to stale in

---

ginning of the last century did their best work when they were very young men,
and questions followed as to why this was so, — why, apparently, it was inevitable. Sargent said that he entirely understood it; that in his own case his inventive power was at its height when he was still a young man and had begun
to decline even in his later twenties. One of the group said, "You don't mean
that your best work is that of your early twenties?" "No," said Sargent, "I
didn't say that. What I said was, my inventive power was at its height in my
first years. As that waned I had to offset the loss of it by an increase of critical
judgment in the selection and treatment of my subjects. On the whole I think
that by so doing I more than compensated over the passing years for the loss of
creative power, and that some of my latest works are also the best. But the
process by which they were achieved was not that of sheer invention, for that
faculty, with the artist, begins to flag very early."

him, Wordsworth was able in 1797–98 to compensate for the loss of early invention by his choice and treatment of subjects. He chose novel subjects, which made him at once an object of interest and controversy, and he treated them in such a manner as to win for himself a permanent place in English letters.

This delayed springtime might seem to have augured for Wordsworth an autumn harvest of better verse than is usually reaped by aging poets. Probably the exact reverse is the truth; for in matters of the mind, as in matters of the body, a skill that is mastered only in the late twenties or the early thirties never becomes second nature. Such techniques require conscious attention and lack the spontaneity of a habit formed at a time when body and mind are supple and as yet in the making. The wonder is that at twenty-seven Wordsworth was able to do so well with a poetic method which he had only then defined to himself.

For all its essential nobility there is in much of Wordsworth's best verse a hint of mental rigidity, a felt want of flexibility. It lacks the unself-consciousness of youth. The noblest numbers achieve a mature majesty of which youth is incapable, but there is little of the margin of poetic high spirits which we find in the earliest and often the best verse of other poets. A certain stiffness to the point of rigidity suggests a man who had mastered his craft too late for his own good. Instead of promising a longer poetic life than normal for Wordsworth, his late arrival must have prophesied a briefer life. The mature self-consciousness employed in the experimental *Lyrical Ballads*, so far from being the sign of genius gathering power, is the mark of an invention already beginning to decline. Thus, if we follow our first thought and say that Wordsworth ought to have written good verse ten years later than the average poet, because he started ten years after that poet, we are probably wrong. Our second thought satisfies us that his poetic life was shortened just because he was so slow in finding himself as a poet. Ideally, the *Lyrical Ballads* should have come a decade sooner.

Both Wordsworth and Dorothy gave to their contemporaries the strong suggestion of having grown old before their time.[1] In his gossip about the poets of the Lake School De Quincey tells us that at the time he knew them best both the poet and his sister seemed spent:

> Some people, it is notorious, live faster by much than others, the oil is burned out sooner in one constitution than in another; and the cause of this may be various; but in the Wordsworths one part of the cause is no doubt, a secret fire of temperament too fervid; the self-consuming energies of the brain that gnaw at the life strings forever. . . . There was in both such a premature expression of old age, that strangers invariably supposed them fifteen or twenty years older than they were.

De Quincey goes on to say that Wordsworth at thirty-eight was once mistaken for over sixty. Plainly there is in his decline a physiological factor to be reckoned with; less piquant perhaps than the emotional and the ethical factors, but none the less pertinent. The whole question of Wordsworth's dates is one which has been ignored and which ought to be reviewed. If De Quincey's testimony is to be trusted, and there is no reason to doubt it, we have a man who was nervously burnt out at forty. He had spent the bulk of his poetic patrimony. His best work had not been begun until he was twenty-seven or twenty-eight, and the fecundity of the next ten years proved costly to his energies. Wordsworth's anti-climax deserves diagnosis not merely at the hands of the psychiatrist and the casuist, but at the hands also of one initially wiser than both, the general medical practitioner![2] The headaches, the ex-

1. Mrs. Threkeld and her daughter, Elizabeth, give, in 1805, "a sad account of poor Dorothy, who is grown so thin and old that they should not have known her." She was, then, thirty-four.
2. Miss Edith Batho, in *The Later Wordsworth* (New York: Macmillan Com-

haustion, the weariness of hand to the point of near-paralysis, are not to be ignored.

To turn, now, to another aspect of our riddle. It has been the fashion of recent years to attribute Wordsworth's poetic decline to his break with Coleridge. The inference is that, as their first friendship had flowered in verse of great beauty, an uninterrupted companionship would have continued to yield for many years profuse blossom of the same quality. As Coleridge had been the first cause, if not the actual author, of Wordsworth's best verse, so he might have continued in that office had the friendship remained inviolate. But after their parting — so runs the critical reflection — Wordsworth was helpless and relapsed into uninspired ventures which were an occasion for his talent but not for his genius.[1]

The open break came in 1810. Coleridge had gone to lodge with the Montagus, and for his friend's good as for their good, Wordsworth had warned them that, because of his habits, Coleridge might prove a difficult lodger. Montagu had found the warning warranted by the event, and in a moment of exasperation had repeated to Coleridge what he remembered Wordsworth to have said. When the first bitterness was past the moot point which remained was this, — had Wordsworth said that Coleridge "had rotted out his entrails" with drugs? Wordsworth denied the precise words, though admitting their substance. He did recall having said that, when Schiller's "body was opened up his entrails were, as it were, eaten up," and he

pany, 1933), pp. 318 ff., suggests that Wordsworth was from a very early time the victim of trachoma, and that this disease progressively deprived him of sight for writing as well as for reading. This may have been so. But since Wordsworth often dictated his poems the brief is not convincing as an extenuation of his later work. Moreover, what of Milton in his blindness?

1. H. W. Garrod, op. cit., p. 30: "If there was any medicine for the decline of power which stole over Wordsworth's poetry after 1807, it was perhaps to be sought from Coleridge. . . . It is hardly an accident that the period of the decline of power coincided with the period in which Wordsworth's gradual estrangement from Coleridge began."

suspected that this vigorous statement had been confused with his diagnosis of Coleridge.

As for Coleridge, he carried the scars of the hurt through all his latter years. If our common sense exonerates Wordsworth, our sympathies go out to Coleridge. His letters betray the depth of the wound:

> I must commence by telling you, great a weakness as it must appear, that so deep and so rankling is the wound, which Wordsworth has wantonly and without the slightest provocation inflicted in return for fifteen year's most enthusiastic self-despising and alas! self-injuring Friendship, (for as to his wretched agents, the Montagus, Carlisles, Knapps, etc., I despise them too much to be seriously hurt by anything, they for themselves can say or do) that I cannot return to Grasmere or its vicinity.
>
> (April, 1811)

> Meantime . . . what with the never-closing festering wound of Wordsworth and his family. . . . (October, 1811)

> The Grasmere business has kept me in a fever of agitation, and will end in complete alienation: I have refused to go over and Wordsworth has refused to apologize. (March, 1812)

> Had I been aware that Mr. Wordsworth's Poem had been announced publicly — for it is now many years since I have been in correspondence with him by letters. (April, 1819)

But Wordsworth had long foreseen the break. The unhappy incident of 1810 only gave semi-public acknowledgment to a fact which he had already accepted. As far as he was concerned the friendship had been imperiled for four or five years prior, because of Coleridge's inability or unwillingness to profit by the help which the poet and Dorothy tried to give him. They had loaned him money, which was never repaid; they had made plans for his good, which had gone astray from the start. The sources, whether journals, letters, or verse, all suggest that Coleridge had made it increasingly hard for Wordsworth and Dorothy to hold his confidence. Meanwhile it is clear that his wife's jealousy kept Coleridge more and more apart from the friends at Grasmere. His absences, growing longer as the years passed, must have been the price he paid for what little peace he had at home. Words in a letter to his wife suggest far more than they say, "Depend on it my dear Wife! that the more you sympathize with me in my kind manners and kind feelings to those at Grasmere the more I shall be likely to sympathize with you in your opinions respecting their faults and imperfections."

Yet as late as the spring of 1806 we find the Wordsworths unable to settle the matter of a new home until Coleridge, who was still included in their plans, returned from Malta. He reached England in August of that year, but lingered on in London before coming to Coleorton, whither the Wordsworths had moved. When he arrived "he was utterly changed. . . . He then scarcely ever spoke of anything that concerned him, or us, or our common friends." [1] He soon left them, apparently unable to endure the condemnation of his own conscience, which charged him in their society with his changed character. It must have been just after this parting that Wordsworth accepted and recorded the fact in verse. English poetry has no finer tribute to friendship achieved and no more tender elegy to friendship lost than is to be found in *A Complaint* (1806).

> There is a change — and I am poor;
> Your love hath been, nor long ago,
> A fountain at my fond heart's door,
> Whose only business was to flow;
> And flow it did: not taking heed
> Of its own bounty, or my need.
>
> What happy moments did I count!
> Blest was I then all bliss above!
> Now, for that consecrated fount
> Of murmuring, sparkling, living love,

---

1. D. W. to Mrs. Clarkson, November 6, 1806.

What have I? shall I dare to tell?
A comfortless and hidden well.

A well of love — it may be deep —
I trust it is, — and never dry:
What matter? if the waters sleep
In silence and obscurity.
— Such change, and at the very door
Of my fond heart, hath made me poor.

Plainly Wordsworth felt bereft as a man and apprehensive as an artist. Without the troubling of the waters by his friend he feared lest the spring of verse in him might dry up. It is no accident that the *Complaint*, with its note of apprehension, was written in the year which saw also the great *Ode: Intimations of Immortality*. The period is that marking the end of the golden decade. Who knows whether the fear itself may not have had a stultifying effect on the poet's genius? In his poem he gave to later critics full warrant for finding in the break with Coleridge the major cause of his decline.

Meanwhile the trouble was of some years' standing. As early as 1803 the substance of the Alfoxden trinity — William, Dorothy, and Coleridge — was in process of being confounded and its persons put to confusion. On the 14th of August in that year the three started gaily on their Scotch tour, but within a fortnight Coleridge had left the other two. Dorothy is gentle in the *Recollections*; Coleridge was not well, could not stand the wet weather in an open carriage, and set off direct for Edinburgh. Nevertheless she and William kept crossing his path in the course of their wanderings, and it looks as though he had been more concerned to get away from them than to reach the city. Shortly after we find him complaining in letters to Poole that Wordsworth was indolent, mired in "self-involution"; "benetted in hypochondriacal Fancies." "I now see very little of Wordsworth." That was toward the end of the year 1803. The unhappy misun-

derstanding over the "rotted entrails" seems to have
been the climax of a considerable period of mutual distrust and criticism.

Let us examine the assumption that had this friendship
continued uninterrupted over further years Wordsworth's
genius would have had a longer life.

William Wordsworth is in many ways a baffling figure;
he does not fit the common categories. He was strangely
wanting in the power of abstract thought and curiously
dependent upon others to supply him with the stuff of his
speculations. He was accused in his lifetime of trafficking
in systems and philosophies tricked out as poems, but
these were seldom or never of his own devising. His systems were borrowed clothes and betray a foreign quality
wherever they appear in his work.

On the other hand, Wordsworth seems not to have had
initially the poet's power to see concrete facts, that is,
to see them poetically. His youthful work abounds in
faithful descriptions, but the insight which makes the
later poems what they are is wanting in his early descriptive sketches; that work is description, not poetry.
He was dependent upon some mind more philosophical
than his own to point out to him the fact at which as
a poet he should look. Once his gaze had been directed
to it and fixed upon it, he could make it yield a poem.
But apparently he had to wait for the speculative thinker
to tell him what to look for in the world of concrete
things.

The only one of Wordsworth's systems which has any
interest today is that which deals with the origin of poems.
Its theses were derived from the associationist psychology
of the day and from the canons of the then dominant English "School of Taste." Wordsworth must have been
familiar with both before he met Coleridge. Johnson's
publishing house in London, which was one of his sanctu-
aries in 1793 and 1794, produced works in these fields.

At a later time Coleridge's fiery transcendentalism was added to Wordsworth's speculative material, and the result was fused by interminable talk into a congruous whole. Having elaborated their system, the two friends immediately set to work to write poems in vindication of it. Their "experiments" were published as the *Lyrical Ballads*.

Thereafter the two men seem to part company mentally. Coleridge lacked the power of concentrated and consecutive thought. He was versatile; he was always suggestive; he had in many ways far the more powerful mind; yet he was desultory. "The man rambled brilliantly," said Crabb Robinson after hearing one of his public lectures, "he is absolutely incorrigible, but his *vitia* are indeed *splendid*." Wordsworth, on the contrary, was a man of dogged ways. His mind, once it had laid hold of an idea, could not release its hold until all the bearings of the idea had been explored and exhausted. Witness his conscientiousness in examining thoroughly and then in finally discarding the superficial system of Godwin. That single intellectual adventure cost him three or four precious years, with little or no profit in the end. The system elaborated with Coleridge's aid had more substance, — after a century it still remains one of the classic theories of poetry, — and to its vindication Wordsworth devoted the best years of his productive life. If he wasted three years on Godwinism, he invested ten years to good purpose in his experiments with the theory of poetry which had been struck off in those interminable walks and talks around Racedown and Alfoxden. Indeed, to the very last, the theory remained the only one by which Wordsworth professed to write, and at the end of the golden decade it had assumed for him the dignity of an article of faith.

The traditional dogma suggests that Wordsworth would have continued to produce great poetry so long as his friendship with Coleridge lasted. The dogma demands a

William Wordsworth who never existed. It requires of him
a versatility which he wholly lacked. He did succeed in
giving a local habitation and a name to the system which
he professed and within which he labored. It took him
years to do so, and while he was so employed he could not
be diverted. Whatever other debt of gratitude we owe to
Wordsworth, we owe him a debt beyond our power of pay-
ment for a brooding conscientiousness which yielded us
noble poems in vindication of the joint theory of poetry.
The theory may be declared false, but if so, not on the
ground of interior inconsistencies. It can be declared false
today only if the poems which were produced in accordance with it are declared failures. Precisely because these
poems, so far from being failures, are an indubitable success we are prohibited from dismissing the system as negli-
gible. If then, as seems probable, we owe the final drafting
of the system to Coleridge, we owe its demonstration to
Wordsworth.

Wordsworth's mind was not the sort required by the
theory that he might have gone on writing good verse if
the fountain of Coleridge's friendship had continued to
flow freely at his door. We cannot imagine Wordsworth
and Coleridge, let us say in 1806 or 1808, when the permutations and combinations of the theory of poetry elaborated in 1798 had been exhausted, joining forces for a
second partnership in some volume of a quite different
nature. Coleridge could have supplied the speculative half
of such a second venture — "Oft, like a winged spider, I
am entangled in a new spun web, but never fear for me,
'tis but the flutter of my wings, and I am off again!" —
but it was not in Wordsworth's power to be thus versatile.
On the contrary, the systematic webs which he spun for
himself were so tough that he was more or less permanently entangled in them.

The truth is that by one of those happy accidents which
from time to time occur Wordsworth and Coleridge met at

a moment when each could do very much for the other.[1]
The one needed further clarification of his thinking, the
other needed the steadying influence of a character more
stable than his own. Like all good things in life the fruits
of that meeting rest in their own right. Conscious attempts
to repeat the initial experience must have failed. In the
mating and parting of these minds there was something
akin to the instinctive processes of nature. By the time
they had left Somerset to go to Germany, Wordsworth and
Coleridge had done, each for the other, all that was humanly possible. Their separation soon after they reached
Hamburg — Wordsworth to go on to Goslar and Coleridge
to Ratzeburg — seems in retrospect a tacit admission
which each made to himself, though not to the other, that
the process of intellectual cross-fertilization had been completed, never to be resumed in its first passionateness. In-
tuitively they must have known that a second *Ancient
Mariner* and a second *Tintern Abbey*, bound within the
covers of another joint volume, were not in the order of
nature.

It is true that in the tenth book of *The Prelude* Wordsworth apostrophizes Coleridge warmly as "my own beloved Friend," and even says of the trip to Malta,

> To me the grief confined that Thou art gone.

But these generous protestations are tempered by a salutary reminder that all is not well with the exile:

> Thine be those motions strong and sanative,
> A ladder for thy Spirit to reascend
> To health and joy and pure contentedness.

---

1. Cf. *The Quarterly Review*, LXV (1840), 234, "It is singular to observe in
how many great revolutions, which have altered the course of human opinions
and affairs, the impulse and direction has been given, not by one but by two
minds, cooperating together, one representing the higher power of the intellect,
and the other more feeling. Plato and Aristotle, Luther and Melancthon, Jerome
and Augustine, Cranmer and Ridley were yoke fellows of this kind; so Wordsworth, the kind, gentle, affectionate Wordsworth, seems to have been almost
paired with the acute, restless, deep-thinking Coleridge."

The *Complaint*, which came two years later, was already in process.

Aside, then, from Wordsworth's own dread lest the loss of Coleridge's friendship might first still the surface waters and finally dry up the springs of his genius — and we have no way of knowing how far this insidious fear may have reacted upon his self-assurance — there is no reason to suppose that the break between the two friends, begun quite unconsciously at Hamburg and finally forced upon them both as a sorry reality in 1810, cost Wordsworth his productive power or in any way caused his poetic decline.

Common sense and conscience forbid us to take exception to Wordsworth's conduct. He was ready and anxious to help Coleridge as long as Coleridge was willing to be helped. It was Coleridge's misfortune — a sick man rather than a bad man — to become increasingly aware of his failings when in the company of the Wordsworths. On Wordsworth's side there never had been the self-abandonment in friendship which Coleridge had showed. Wordsworth was too cautious, too preoccupied, too self-centered to be capable of such generosity of mind and heart. His very correctness must have nettled the more sensitive Coleridge. We absolve William — and we doubly absolve Dorothy and Mary — of the least lack of considerate charity at any point between 1797 and 1810, yet had Wordsworth been a man of more impulsive nature, the difficulties might have been surmounted.

Crabb Robinson eventually effected a formal and public reconciliation, but the private wounds were never healed. To the last Wordsworth was careful to acknowledge his debt to his friend, but he was much too honest to pretend that personal relations had been restored in their prior intimacy. Our sympathies go out, rather, to Coleridge, who after all the bitterness could still write (1828) with something of his first affection, "So only give my best love to Mr. and Mrs. Wordsworth, and Miss Wordsworth."

CHAPTER IV

The French Revolutionist

IN THE poet's lifetime his literary decline was charged
to his change of political opinions. The critics assumed that conservatism is not as promising seed-
ground for verse as radicalism, and there is something
to be said for the assumption. Poets have usually been un-
conventional persons, and orthodoxy is seldom lyric. Here
is Crabb Robinson's account of the falling-off, which he
had marked and deplored. He writes to Dorothy (February 20, 1826):

It is a sort of moral & intellectual suicide in your brother not
to have continued his admirable series of poems 'dedicated to
liberty' he might add And 'public virtue.' (I assure you it gives
me real pain when I think that some future commentator may
possibly hereafter write 'This great poet survived to the fifth
decennary of the nineteenth Century, but he appears to have
dyed in the year 1814 as far as life consisted in an active sympathy with the temporary welfare of his fellow creatures — He
had written heroically & divinely against the tyranny of Napoleon, but was quite indifferent to all the successive tyrannies
which disgraced the succeeding times —) The Spaniards the
moment they were under the yoke of the most odious & con-
temptible tyrant that ever breathed — ceased to be objects of
interest — the Germans who emancipated themselves were
most ungratefully neglected by their sovereigns & the poet —
the Greeks began a War as holy as that of the Spaniards He
was silent — He had early manifested a feeling for the negroes
& the poet did honour to his friend Clarkson — That source of
sympathetic tears was dried up — A new field of enterprise was
opened in America — the poets eye was not a prophetic one —

There is proof that he was alive about 1823–4 when the new churches were built in London but otherwise he took no care about any of the events of the day.

The good Robinson's fears were not unwarranted. Twenty-five years later, this was precisely what posterity had begun to say of Wordsworth. A survey of his life and work, published just after his death, labors the point which Crabb Robinson had foreseen:

The creative power of Wordsworth would appear to have been paralyzed after the publication of the *Excursion*. All his most finished works precede that period. . . . The main secret of the freezing up of his fountain of political inspiration, we really take to have been his change of politics. Wordsworth's muse was essentially liberal — one may say, Jacobinical. That he was unconscious of any sordid motive for his change, we sincerely believe; but certainly his conforming was the result less of reasonable conviction than of wilfulness. It was by a determined effort of his will that he brought himself to believe in the church-and-state notions which he latterly promulgated. Hence the want of definite views and of a living interest, which characterizes all his writings subsequent to that change, when compared with those of an earlier time.

In the 1890's "Mark Rutherford" attempted to acquit Wordsworth of the charge of political apostasy,[1] and during the war Professor Dicey came gratefully to Wordsworth's defense as having been not only consistent in his political thinking but prophetic of England's foreign policy during all the latter half of the nineteenth century.[2] Such books would not have been pertinent at their late dates were it not that the suspicion of political treason lingered on to cast its shadow over the poet's reputation. Presumably

1. William Hale White, *An Examination of the Charge of Apostasy against Wordsworth* (London: Longmans, Green, and Company, 1898).
2. A. V. Dicey, *The Statesmanship of Wordsworth* (Oxford: Clarendon Press, 1917).

Browning's *Lost Leader* had done much to confirm the suspicion.

There are two issues here: first, how far Wordsworth's change of political affiliation affected his powers as a poet; second, to what extent and in what manner he was a politically-minded man?

We are asked, on the hypothesis in question, to believe that Wordsworth, the French revolutionary, was a great poet and Wordsworth, the English Tory, a bad poet. His genius, we are to gather, was killed by the creeping paralysis of political conservatism. The theory has become so much a critical convention that we do not realize how few facts can be mustered to support it. We have bad verse, and to spare, from the Tory years, but we have almost no verse from the revolutionary years. The only poems of importance prior to the *Lyrical Ballads* are *An Evening Walk*, *Descriptive Sketches*, *The Borderers*, and *Guilt and Sorrow*. The last two were written while the poet was under the spell of Godwin, and seem to have been an attempt to make some sort of peace with himself after his return from France.[1] They are not primarily concerned with political matters, though their argument may have a political reference. But *An Evening Walk* and *Descriptive Sketches* were published immediately after the poet's return to England in 1793, and while he still professed the republican faith. If we attempt to defend the theory that Wordsworth the youthful revolutionary wrote good poetry, the case must be made on the strength of these two short works. The former had been on the stocks for five or six years and antedated the revolutionary period. The latter, however, had been composed in France while Wordsworth was supposedly aflame with revolutionary zeal. *Descrip-*

1. But cf. "Date of Composition of *The Borderers*," *Modern Language Notes*, XLIX (1934), 104; and "Genesis of *The Borderers*," *PMLA*, XLIX (1934), 922. According to these papers *The Borderers* was not begun until the autumn of 1796, when the "strong disease" of Godwinism was already over.

tive Sketches was dedicated to Robert Jones and was intended to recall for him, as to record for others, the impressions of their trip in 1790. At the same time it brought those impressions down to date on the strength of the poet's more recent experiences in Blois and Orleans. The Revolution, nascent when Jones and he had gone to France, was in full force when he wrote in 1791–92. The stirring events of the moment furnish a part of the subject-matter of this work. Yet there is about his references to the Revolution as Wordsworth enters them in the *Descriptive Sketches* — and we should remember that this is the only contemporary record in verse which he gave us — a curious dispassionateness.

> Oh give, great God, to Freedom's waves to ride
> Sublime o'er Conquest, Avarice, and Pride. . . .
> — Give them beneath their breast while Gladness springs,
> To brood the Nations o'er with Nile-like wings.

A devout and proper wish, but not political propaganda likely to foment a revolution. In spite of sympathy with the event, there is a reflective detachment. Wordsworth was viewing the action as one above its battles. Of their kind the lines are good poetry, but as poetry they are not as good as "and never lifted up a single stone"; nor are they characteristic of Wordsworth at his best. They are examples of an abstract moralizing in meter which he could do well at any time in his life. They would not have been out of character after the golden decade, but they do not make a case for high excellence before that decade.

The poet's best work is that which began in 1797–98, and by then he was well on the way to being cured of France and all it had meant to him. When in 1802 he finally addressed himself to his own country in the noble sonnets which celebrate English liberty and the English tradition, he does so with a literary power which no prior account of the Revolution had evoked from him. In their particular vein these sonnets, which follow along until the end of the Napoleonic Wars, have never been equaled. They stand alone in the poetry of patriotism, as we know it in English letters.

Whether the sonnets on England deserve to be called political poems is another question. They are freighted with love of country, but love of country is a complex emotion, and is not always a matter of political theory held with zeal. It is quite as often a matter of felt kinship with a familiar scene, a yearning of our clay to the clay of the pit whence it is digged. English patriotism has been far more often a matter of strong sentiment for the well-loved countryside than of subscription to an abstract theory of the state. "Dear earth, I do salute thee" is its constant theme. Wordsworth as a boy had felt that emotion, though he had not defined it. After his return from France the feeling eventually reasserted itself, became known for what it was, and remained the essence of his love of England. Indeed, he says in so many words that "local attachment is the tap-root of the tree of Patriotism." [1]

When Wordsworth turned from his affection for the land and for people who lived near the land to a concern for England's public weal, he did not write as a politician or even as a statesman. He wrote as one of the old Hebrew prophets might have written:

> Milton! thou shouldst be living at this hour:
> England hath need of thee: she is a fen
> Of stagnant waters: altar, sword, and pen,
> Fireside, the heroic wealth of hall and bower,
> Have forfeited their ancient English dower
> Of inward happiness. We are selfish men;
> Oh! raise us up, return to us again;
> And give us manners, virtue, freedom, power.
> Thy soul was like a Star and dwelt apart.

---

1. William Knight, *Prose Works of William Wordsworth* (London: Macmillan and Company, 1896), II, 187.

In the later years there were ungenerous and reactionary verses, addressed to interior changes in the structure of English society. At the time of the passage of the Reform Bill Wordsworth breathed out the most dire Jeremiads. The bill itself he described as "a greater political crime than any in history."[1] As for the constitution of England, he thought it was "about to be destroyed,"[2] and "as to public affairs, I have no hope but in the goodness of Almighty God."[3] The facts seemed to him capable of only one interpretation: the people were "bent upon the destruction of their ancient institutions."[4] As for the future, "Nothing I am persuaded will bring this Nation back to its senses. And when it recovers, then it will be a long time under the necessity of sacrificing liberty to order, probably under a military government but at least under one unavoidably despotic."[5]

The poet's friends were unimpressed. Crabb Robinson wrote to his brother, "Wordsworth is an alarmist. The great difference between him & me is that he is a *despairing* and I am a *hoping* alarmist."[6] With the passage of time Wordsworth's fears were slowly dispelled, and he became more tolerant of changes which at the moment he could not understand. It was Crabb Robinson's conviction that Wordsworth was "by nature a liberal, tho accidents have cast him among the adversaries."[7] As for the poet himself, he was unequivocal in stating his reasons for dissenting from the Reform movement. "It is a fixed judgement of my mind that an unbridled democracy is the worst of all tyrannies."[8] The opinion was not hastily formed, it was

1. W. W. to Lord Lonsdale, February 17, 1832.
2. W. W. to William Rowan Hamilton, November 22, 1831.
3. W. W. to Lady Frederick Bentinck, November 9, 1831.
4. W. W. to H. C. R., November 15, 1833.
5. W. W. to H. C. R., May 5, 1833.
6. H. C. R. to T. R., July 4, 1833.
7. H. C. R. to T. R., December 23, 1847.
8. W. W. to H. C. R., February 5, 1833.

his sober conclusion after watching the French Revolution run its course. No one can say that it was wholly without warrant, and Wordsworth was not the first, nor will he be the last, to doubt whether "unbridled democracy" is the final word in political wisdom.

We should remember, also, that Wordsworth's interest in political affairs had been addressed at the outset to events on the Continent. His early interest in English public life was subordinate to a prior concern for the fortunes of the idea of freedom in France. Many of his later sonnets and shorter poems on Continental politics follow their fluctuations through subsequent years. But by the time the Napoleonic Wars were ended the situation in Europe defied treatment in poetry. Wordsworth attempted it in the *Thanksgiving Ode* (1816), but the poem was felt at the time not to be successful. A contemporary reviewer pointed out the inherent impossibility of the task; the happenings with which this ode deals were "on too large a scale for the imagination to comprehend." What was much more to the point, England herself lacked the spiritual unity which might have made such a poem a faithful transcript of the national mind:

> The errors and crimes of different governments . . . the whole system of European policy, for the last twenty years, may with much reason excite, on the retrospect, sentiments of a painful and indignant nature. It is not to be forgotten, that the contests in which during that period this country has been engaged, have not all been with a military despot; have not all been a struggle between good and evil principles. We have loved war better than peace, our policy being evil, and we are now reaping the bitter, bitter fruits of that unnatural excitation which war occasions. The victory of Waterloo was achieved by a last desperate effort of feverish strength; it has left us without an enemy, but it has also left us impoverished, spiritless, in the weakness of exhaustion. . . . We do not believe that the poet exists, who could succeed in making war, as a present event, interesting to the imagination. . . . Loyalty devoid of affection, patriotism

destitute of virtue, triumph without joy and hope without confidence cannot give you good poetry.[1]

We need only substitute its modern equivalent for the reviewer's "Waterloo" to have in the passage a painfully faithful account of the dilemma of the modern poet who addresses himself to the present world situation. No political poetry, dealing with the total stage, has been possible since 1918. Poetry cannot compass the diverse facts, and a want of spiritual integrity in the modern world frustrates at the outset the attempt to interpret them poetically. Poetry requires a concrete subject and a unified inner life. We lack both, as Wordsworth and his age lacked them after Waterloo. When Wordsworth turned away from Continental affairs which had got out of hand and addressed himself to the sorry task of resisting economic and electoral reforms at home, he admitted that his ideal had eluded him. He had expected domestic reforms in England, as in France, to follow as corollaries of the vindication of the principle of liberty. He lacked the patient temper of the reformer who is willing to take a quarter of a loaf when he cannot get the whole loaf. His reluctance to concern himself in behalf of the slaves and to join the abolition movement perplexed his friends. On his part, he had assumed that if the cause of liberty prevailed slavery would go. Having been disappointed in the larger hope he had little heart for such fragments as could be salvaged. He lacked the kind of mind which knows how to get ashore on broken pieces of the ship. Hence his failure to manifest in behalf of the humaner political movements of his later life the passion which he had entertained for a bolder ideal at an earlier time.

The only strictly political poetry in Wordsworth, worked out to any length, is that found in the closing books of *The Prelude*. As poetry it is neither so good as Words-

1. *The Eclectic Review, New Series*, VI (1816), 16.

worth's best verse nor so bad as his worst. It is at least well above the mid-line. If its indifferent excellence is to be attributed to its subject, its defects may quite as possibly be attributed to the attitude which at the time of writing Wordsworth took toward his subject. He was trying to recover a past self with which he had consciously broken. The break put him out of sympathy with his former self, yet this self had been so vivid that he could not deny it or dismiss it from memory. In spite of oncoming British conservatism, he could still write of his republican years with a certain power. When, therefore, we speak of Wordsworth as a political poet, in distinction from Wordsworth the patriot, we are restricted by that phrase to the last five books of *The Prelude* in which he describes the Revolution, his own part in it, and his parting from it. Otherwise there is little political verse in his best work.

Renan used to say that no one can give an accurate account of religion who has not himself been a religious man, but that he cannot describe a religion accurately while he still professes it. To do so he must first have professed it, then have left it. This often-quoted dictum has affinities with Wordsworth's theory of the genesis of poetry. He held that no man can make poetic use of an emotion, and thus of the insights given by the emotion, while it is strong on him. Such an emotion must be recollected in tranquillity. As he looked back upon his own past he said,

> so wide appears
> The vacancy between me and those days,
> Which yet have such self-presence in my mind
> That, sometimes, when I think of them, I seem
> Two consciousnesses, conscious of myself
> And of some other Being.

Wordsworth was probably right in thinking that he could give poetic expression to himself only as he stood outside his own past.

On this theory it is fair to say that *The Prelude*, composed after he had made the break with France, is probably a more faithful transcript of his revolutionary period than are the scattered contemporary references to the event found in the *Descriptive Sketches*. He was, at the time *The Prelude* was being written, wholly committed to the theories of art which had been elaborated in the preface to the second edition of the *Lyrical Ballads*. There is not the slightest reason to suppose that when he turned from poems about natural objects and simple human lives to the history of his own mind Wordsworth consciously adopted or was forced to adopt unconsciously another poetic method. He concedes that he cannot avoid imputing something of his mature mind to his youth and early manhood — no autobiographer has ever been able to do otherwise. Nevertheless, his peculiar power to recollect past emotions accurately cannot have been in abeyance in the writing of his great autobiography.

You cannot have it both ways in reading *The Prelude*. You cannot treat it as a work of casuistries and sophistries, disclosing an insincerity that its author was attempting to conceal from himself as from others, and at the same time use it as a reliable source-book for the mining of facts with which it professes to deal. Much modern criticism of Wordsworth errs flagrantly in this respect, using the poem variously as a masterpiece of self-deception in maturity and as a dependable source for accurate information about the early years.

At some time between 1805, when he wrote the story of *Vaudracour and Julia* as a part of *The Prelude*, and 1820, when he published the story separately, Wordsworth decided not to run the risk of laying the tale open to the autobiographical interpretation which it invited in its original setting. He was probably ill-advised in the matter, since his prudence has had the effect of making us doubt the candor of *The Prelude* in its entirety. Yet this single act of discretion is the only cause we have for doubting the honesty of *The Prelude*, and, though we may think that Wordsworth would have been wiser to have left his love poem where he first placed it, we should remember that the total quality of *The Prelude* was not changed by his act of editorial caution.

Apart from this omission there is little reason to suppose that Wordsworth has not given us in *The Prelude* as faithful a transcript of his early life as is humanly possible. In recreating, under more tranquil circumstances, the emotions which he had felt from 1790 to 1795 he probably came nearer the truth than he could have come at that earlier time. *The Prelude* opens with the blunt statement,

> I breathe again;
> Trances of thought and mountings of the mind
> Come fast upon me: it is shaken off,
> That burthen of my own unnatural self,
> The heavy weight of many a weary day.

We have here either the beginning of the long-sustained hypocrisy or the truth. I cannot resist the conclusion that the lines are substantially true, and that the poet never felt the French Revolution as a personal concern. William Wordsworth until he was nearly thirty was like a ship waiting for a steady breeze. At times he was becalmed and without steerage way, at other times he was blown about by gentle catspaws or by sudden gusts; he had not picked up the wind which should carry him on his destined course. Nothing is plainer than the casualness, the vacillation, the indecision, of the years from childhood through the school and university days, on into the desultory months in London and the distracted years in France. Always at the back of his mind was the hope that

> I might leave
> Some monument behind me which pure hearts
> Should reverence.

But neither the theme nor the inspiration nor the technique was given.

No critic has ever questioned the accuracy of the poet's statement about Cambridge,

> A feeling that I was not for that hour
> Nor for that place.

Nor has anyone ventured to suggest that Wordsworth was a lost leader to the world of academic things because he decided not to become a don. In retrospect he puts both Cambridge and France under common condemnation in identical words; they were "not mine." Either Wordsworth is lying or he is telling the truth, a truth deeply felt in both scenes, an intuition rather than a reasoned confidence that

> all my deeper passions lay elsewhere.

Whether William Wordsworth would have been a more admirable character had he cast in his lot with the French Girondins and

> A poor mistaken and bewilder'd offering,
> Should to the breast of Nature have gone back

is a purely academic question. English poetry would have been immeasurably the poorer had he chosen thus, and it is difficult to see wherein France would have profited, though he played with the idea that a single man may greatly affect the course of history and that he might have been to the republican cause such a man. But a Wordsworth who could have chosen thus would have been a Wordsworth other than the one with whom we have to come to terms. We are dealing with a man who for years had been persuaded that he was a dedicated poet, though the hour of his advent tarried.

His faith in his call to poetry ruled all his personal choices, and led him to leave France and to get on with his

mission.[1] His return to England was not cowardice, it was
not vanity, it was consent to a foreordination and election
to art which determined his life. The results of his faith, in
the terms of the yield of the golden decade, prove that it
was not illusory. Save that the event would have been less
dramatic, we might as well blame Wordsworth for not becoming a Cambridge don as for failing to get himself executed on a French guillotine. He refused both destinies
for the same reason; he could not conceive them as his.

Meanwhile, Wordsworth had never been converted to
the doctrines of the Revolution, because he had no need to
be. Its major ideas had been the uncriticized axioms of his
whole life. He took democracy for granted; it was the only
life he had ever known:

> For, born in a poor District, and which yet
> Retaineth more of ancient homeliness,
> Manners erect, and frank simplicity,
> Than any other nook of English Land,
> It was my fortune scarcely to have seen
> Through the whole tenor of my School-day time
> The face of one, who, whether Boy or Man,
> Was vested with attention or respect
> Through claims of wealth or blood; nor was it least
> Of many debts which afterwards I owed
> To Cambridge, and an academic life
> That something there was holden up to view
> Of a Republic. . . .

When Wordsworth and Jones landed in France in July,
1790, they found themselves welcome and understood:

> we bore a name
> Honour'd in France, the name of Englishmen,
> And hospitably did they give us hail
> As their forerunners in a glorious course.

---

1. There was of course the necessity of providing for Annette, and his funds
had run out. But he proposed to solve the practical problem by writing and
publishing verse.

As for the heady wine of the democratic idea, Wordsworth was too accustomed to it to become intoxicated.
He had grown up in a society which had

> a local soul
> Of independence and stern liberty.

This political patrimony had been fortified by casual reading of tracts which vindicated the rights of the natural
man:

> Like others I had read, and eagerly
> Sometimes, the master Pamphlets of the day.

Wordsworth was a once-born revolutionary who had no
call to be twice-born. He took the ideas of republicanism
for granted, and since they were his second mental nature,
so far from being excited by them, he merely wondered
that they had arrived so late in France. It was a matter
of course with him to rate

> As best the government of equal rights
> And individual worth. And hence, O Friend!
> If at the first great outbreak I rejoiced
> Less than might well befit my youth, the cause
> In part lay here, that unto me the events
> Seemed nothing out of nature's certain course,
> A gift that rather was come late than soon.

In the ninth book of *The Prelude* there is an illuminating
account of Wordsworth's identification with the course of
affairs at Orleans and Blois from November, 1791, until
the end of 1792, when he left Paris to go back to England.
At first he was unconcerned for the Revolution and interested rather in the difference of manners as between England and a French provincial city. Orleans was relatively
quiet in the latter months of '91, and for a time he amused
himself with persons of "privilege of birth" who still observed "punctilios of elegance" and were indifferent to
"deeper causes." Wordsworth, who was hardly at home
in this setting, transferred himself to "a knot of military

Officers," royalists, who were "bent upon undoing what
was done," and who tried incidentally to convert the young
Englishman to their cause. Their potential recruit was
stubborn, having no native interest in "Sceptres, Orders
and Degrees." Meanwhile he watched the youth of
France "posting on to meet the War upon her Frontier
Bounds," and was "still a Stranger."

Then he met Beaupuy — a renegade royalist and a revolutionary. In this relationship we have again an example
of Wordsworth's curious dependence upon another man to
fire his latent enthusiasms. If William Wordsworth ever
believed in the French Revolution, it was at the moment
when Beaupuy pointed to that

> hunger-bitten Girl
> Who crept along, fitting her languid gait
> Upon a Heifer's motion. . . .
> . . . at the sight my Friend
> In agitation said, "'Tis against *that*
> Which we are fighting."

Wordsworth felt the Revolution then. Its principles were
transmuted from second mental nature into a passionate
poetic conviction. The incident marks the zenith of his
sympathy with France. The sight persuaded him that a
time must come when this earth should be

> Unthwarted in her wish to recompense
> The industrious, and the lowly Child of Toil.

But this was essentially an esthetic rather than a political
experience, a swift emotional insight into the truth of a
concrete fact. The passage is moving, even convincing,
but does not discover the stuff of which effective revolutionists are made.

Wordsworth must have been far more faithful to his
dominant interests during 1792 in his description of the
political day-dreaming in which he and Beaupuy indulged.

Oh! sweet it is, in academic Groves,
Or such retirement, Friend! as we have known. . . .
To ruminate with interchange of talk
On rational liberty, and hope in Man. . . .
Such conversation under Attic shades
Did Dion hold with Plato.

The lines lack the smell of gunpowder and blood. There is the same detachment which we noticed in the *Descriptive Sketches*. Wordsworth, in France, was an absolute idealist in political matters, but an idealist who had not attempted to translate his abstractions into fact. He seems to have taken it for granted that some cosmic energy in nature or in history shared his views and would vindicate them. But he was a stranger to what the Russian anarchists of a later time called "the propaganda of the deed." Ten years afterward, back in England, he drilled with the territorial forces which were being recruited to resist a possible invasion by Napoleon's armies, yet one does not think of him as a promising man-at-arms. Meanwhile, in France, he watched Beaupuy go to what was to be his death in defense of the cause. It never occurred to him that he should have gone with his gallant friend; indeed, so far as bearing a hand in the stern world of fact was concerned, he seems to have known only one moment — that, during the latter months of 1792, while he was in Paris — when any such course presented itself to him as a possible path of duty.

William Wordsworth was not a man of action. If he was a revolutionist, he was not the sort of revolutionist from whom an existing order has any violence to fear. He looked to nature to work its own revolutions in men and affairs; he was content to watch the change and to celebrate in verse the increment of social good which he confidently expected. He was as inert in action as Byron was aggressive. Both men were revolutionists, but they wore their rue with a difference. We do not accuse Wordsworth of hypocrisy because he failed in certain instances to show forth with his life the faith which he professed with his lips. He was far too reflective a nature ever to be at ease in the world of affairs, to say nothing of a world of battle, murder, and sudden death. He was in these matters an idealist without guile.

He came back to England either at the very end of 1792 or in the first days of 1793. He had not been home more than a few weeks before England declared war on France, a war which dragged along for ten years until the inconclusive Peace of Amiens. He found himself cut off from France, but with his sympathies still across the Channel rather than in his own country. He had been puzzled, even distressed, by the excesses which he had seen in Paris on his way home, yet he was loyal to the cause. His position, therefore, was both sorry and dangerous. The years from 1793 to the autumn of 1795 were the bitterest of his life. They form another chapter of his story.

CHAPTER V

The English Tory

WHO knows what might have happened to Wordsworth had he stayed in France? Presumably he would have gone to his death with his fellow Girondins. They were a moderate party, soon swamped by the extremists. Paris in 1793 was no place for gentle humanitarians. A reviewer of *The Prelude* gives his imagination rein in reading Wordsworth's own speculations as to his probable fate, had he not gone back to England:

Wordsworth, it appears, the Poet Laureate of England, was once very near . . . dying on a scaffold among the victims of Robespierre. Nay, to make a contrary suggestion, who knows what might have been the value to change the course of history, in a soul so pure as his, poured like a tributary into the revolutionary stream? What questions one might go on to ask. Had Wordsworth carried his dream into effect, would Robespierre have gone on to be precisely the man he was? Might there not have been an arrest for his course in the very fact that this young Englishman was there to watch him? And, more daring suggestion still, may it not have been a *sine qua non* for the future elevation to power of a certain bronze-faced young Corsican then in Paris, that this white-skinned young Englishman, his junior by half a year, should be sent home to his native hills? [1]

A runaway Wordsworth as the occasion for Napoleon is one of the subtler refinements of historical fancy!

1. *The British Quarterly Review*, XII (1850), 572.

Back in England his readjustment to his country and its policies cost him three precious years, which he could ill spare. By the turning of the century he was becoming a Tory. What had the change meant to him and how are we to reinterpret it?

The youthful Wordsworth was a political doctrinaire and his utterances are true to type. Such persons have no feeling for history, because the changeless order of nature in which their ideals are grounded, and by which ideals are vindicated, has no need of either the past or the future. Its realities dwell in an eternal present. There can be no genuine act in such a world.

> Action is transitory — a step, a blow,
> The motion of a muscle — this way or that —
> 'Tis done, and in the after-vacancy
> We wonder at ourselves like men betrayed.

Wordsworth eventually parted company with the political dogmas of naturalism and enlightenment. We find him in due time a convert to an entirely different conception of the state, of citizenship, and of happenings in time. We can identify both the nature of his conversion and its occasion. It is intimated by the inclusion, in the final draft of *The Prelude*, of the passage in praise of Burke which is wanting in the original draft. The prose writings give even more definite information. In his *Letter to the Bishop of Landaff* (1793) Wordsworth writes as an unrepentant republican. In the course of the *Letter* he says:

Mr. Burke roused the indignation of all ranks of men when, by a refinement in cruelty superior to that which in the East yokes the living to the dead he strove to persuade us that we and our posterity to the end of time were riveted to a constitution by the indissoluble compact of — a dead parchment, and were bound to cherish a corpse at the bosom when reason might call aloud that it should be entombed.

By the time he wrote *The Convention of Cintra* (1809)
he had reversed his stand, and we find him saying:

There is a spiritual community binding together the living
and the dead; the good, the brave, and the wise, of all ages. We
would not be rejected from this community: and therefore do we
hope.

He must have come to this conclusion at least four years
earlier, since we have the same idea in the 1805 text of
The Prelude:

There is
One great Society alone on earth,
The noble Living and the noble Dead.

Thereafter the thought was a commonplace with Wordsworth, though these early lines are perhaps its finest statement in his verse. Where did he get the new idea, and
what led him to change his mind? The answer is, Burke.

The reference to Burke in Wordsworth's letter to the
bishop is to be found in Burke's *Reflections on the Revolution in France*. Burke's attitude toward the Revolution
had been outspoken and consistent. He believed in a
monarchy because it was a symbol of the continuity of
national life. He disbelieved in democracy, particularly of
the type lauded in France, because he thought that it was
wanting in a feeling for history, and that no society could
permanently endure without an awareness of national
tradition running through many generations. Burke had
no confidence in the social contract, if that contract was
construed as being so contemporary a fact that it dis-
pensed with a nation's past and future. The passage
which Wordsworth had in mind is one of the most striking
political utterances in English statesmanship:

Society is indeed a contract. Subordinate contracts for objects of mere occasional interest may be dissolved at pleasure —
but the state ought not to be considered as nothing better than

a partnership agreement in a trade of pepper and coffee, callico or tobacco, or some such other low concern, to be taken up for a little temporary interest, and to be dissolved by the fancy of the parties. . . . It is a partnership in all science; a partnership in all art; a partnership in every virtue, and in all perfection. As the ends of such a partnership cannot be obtained in many generations, it becomes a partnership not only between those who are living, but between those who are living, those who are dead, and those who are to be born. Each contract of each particular state is but a clause in the great primeval contract of eternal society . . . connecting the visible and invisible world.

At some time between 1793 and 1805 Wordsworth was made historically-minded by Burke; and, after his conversion to Burke's doctrine of the state a feeling for tradition, reaching over many generations, is evident in all his work. The pretty affectation of antiquity, in which the eighteenth century had indulged, became a confidence in the organic nature of the life of man in a political society.

This is the only radical change in political thinking which Wordsworth ever underwent. One who understands the issues which were at stake cannot think of his conversion to Burke's conception of the state as anything other than a gain. At this distance, we judge the mature Wordsworth to have been a wiser man than the ingenuous youth. To require of him, in the name of consistency, fidelity to a doctrine found wanting at an important point, is to equate idealism with fanaticism. We should not deny to Wordsworth the right to grow up, nor should we deprive him of the wisdom of experience. What is sound truth in Burke cannot be a craven lie in Wordsworth merely because he reached that truth by slow and painful steps.

If further evidence of the strong influence of Burke be needed, we find it in the argument of *The Convention of Cintra*.[1] There is the same plea for a generous understand-

1. Ed. A. V. Dicey, pp. 61 ff.

ing of persons other than insular English which Burke had made in behalf of the misunderstood American colonists. There is the same criticism of practical politicians; they are neither good enough nor astute enough to be intrusted with the care of large affairs. Altogether Wordsworth had read his Burke to good purpose, and we have, once more, a good example of his dependence upon others to clarify for him his abstract thinking.

Were there any other substantial changes in Wordsworth's political thought? I doubt it. A strong case can be made for the contention that Wordsworth remained constant, throughout his life, to the ideals which he professed in his youth.[1] In saying so, however, we should remember that these were political ideals and not political programs. If Wordsworth traded his party affiliations, he did so because he thought his dreams had better chance of fulfilment under Tory than under Whig or Jacobin rule. He never recanted, even in his most conservative period, the conviction that England should not have gone to war with France in 1793. He continued to stand by the principle which he had then affirmed, that the nations of Europe should be allowed the right of self-determination. His stubborn confidence in the French was finally destroyed by their wanton invasion of Switzerland. The Swiss were too nearly akin to his own Lake District shepherds to be subjected to such infringement of their natural rights.

Moreover, the publication of *The Prelude*, for which the poet was prepared and for which he made definite provision, can be construed only as a reaffirmation of faith in his earliest political convictions. The latter books of the work had a difficult and even a compromising story to tell. Prudential considerations would have pointed to their

1. W. W. to Lord Lonsdale, December 4, 1821. *"You* have been deluded by *places* and *persons,* while I have stuck to *principles. I* abandoned France, and her rulers, when *they* abandoned the struggle for liberty, gave themselves up to tyranny, and endeavoured to enslave the world."

suppression rather than to their publication, had not the
poet felt that there were both continuity and consistency
running through the successive stages of his history.
    In his old age Wordsworth said of himself that he had a
good deal of the Chartist in him. He seems to have made
much that impression upon certain of his contemporaries.
Harriet Martineau was left with the persuasion that "his
mind must always have been essentially liberal." A Whig
reviewer of *The Prelude* said, "Despite his own efforts,
Wordsworth is the child and champion of Jacobinism. . . .
Even in the ranks of our opponents Wordsworth has been
laboring in our behalf." And fifty years later "Mark
Rutherford" wrote with penetrating insight, "If Wordsworth had been in the House of Commons, he would
have been considered dangerous, for it is recurrence to
first principles which has produced every great revolution,
whether in religion, morals, politics, or art."
    Wordsworth's middle years were spent in an England
which was entering upon the period of intense industrial-
ism. He never wholly understood the age. The clash between the claims of the agriculturalist and those of the
industrialist has been, for a century, a political and economic fact of the first importance. Their interests have
proved at times to be mutually exclusive and have never
been successfully reconciled. Every man falls, by virtue
of his circumstance, on one side or on the other of the line
which divides the city from the country. Wordsworth's
native sympathies were with the farmer and the shepherd;
he had no experience of mill cities and little prophetic
vision of the England which was to be built up around
them. Yet we do him an injustice if we think that he confined his Utopian visions to his immediate neighbors and
withheld them from the men and women and little children who were beginning to be caught in the machine. In
the latter part of *The Excursion* there are lines in their
behalf, written with as much sympathy, if not with as

much indignation, as *The Song of the Shirt*. In the 1835 *Postscript to the Poetical Works*, we even find him urging the repeal of laws which prohibit the forming of joint-stock companies and pressing for a far more co-operative interpretation of industrial affairs.[1] The poet was still an impenitent republican, not a Tory of the line.

But, in the end, we come back to our initial question, How far was Wordsworth a politically-minded man? He once told the Reverend Orville Dewey (1833) "that although he was known to the world only as a poet, he had given twelve hours of thought to the condition and prospects of society, for one to poetry." There are stray facts to bear out his affirmation. His figure, seen striding over Dunmail Raise in the late hours of the night to meet the post and get the news from France, seems to confirm his statement. Such evidence, backed by certain of the poems, prompts a recent writer to say that Wordsworth is England's greatest political poet after Shakespeare and Milton.[2]

Is it possible that we have drifted into overemphasis, if not overstatement in this matter? Wordsworth became in due time one of England's most devoted lovers. Furthermore, he dealt in many of his poems with contemporary events. Yet neither his love of England nor his interest in European affairs makes him a political thinker of the first rank, and they do not make him a political poet in the ordinary meaning of that word. Wordsworth was political in the sense that the Old Testament prophets were political; he preached the application of broad moral principles to the conduct of affairs of state. He was not a political poet in the sense that either his verse or his prose had the slightest effect on the course of public events. He lived, mentally, too far above the battle to influence its fortunes.

1. *Prose Works of William Wordsworth*, II, 360.
2. Geoffrey L. Bickersteth, *Leopardi and Wordsworth* (Annual Italian Lecture of the British Academy, 1927).

The Prelude is devoted, in part, to an account of events in France from 1790 until the rise of Napoleon. Despite the fact that it was written ten years after the times which it describes, it still remains a valuable source-document, giving us the impressions made by the Revolution upon a powerful mind. But when he deals with "action" which is "transitory" rather than with principles which he supposes to be eternal, Wordsworth is essentially a recorder and an interpreter, not a propagandist.

One has only to consult such of his prose works as were an attempt to exercise a direct influence on public opinion to see how far removed he was from a man like Burke. *The Convention of Cintra* was a morally impassioned tract, but it universalized a particular fact which did not seem to other men as important as it seemed to Wordsworth. Perhaps the truce at Cintra was as ignoble as Wordsworth held it to be, yet at this distance the poet's historical perspective seems poor. Many of us today know of Cintra only through its association with Wordsworth, and even his great authority fails to convince us that its "stain will cleave to the British name as long as the story of this island shall endure." By contrast Burke, and Cobden, and Bright — men of kindred depth of moral passion — have not had to be rewritten to restore a correct historical focus.

As a practical politician in his home counties Wordsworth must have been a pathetic failure. It is hard to imagine a campaign broadside less calculated to make votes than the *Two Addresses to the Freeholders of Westmorland*, published in 1818 when Brougham was trying to supplant the Lonsdale candidate for Parliament. William and Dorothy descended from Rydal upon Kendal and served the Lonsdale cause as door-to-door canvassers, backing the printed addresses with a personal appeal. In a campaign speech Brougham referred slightingly to Wordsworth's political abilities as a pamphleteer. Dorothy says to Sara Hutchinson, "He expected that the mob would at once understand what he alluded to . . . but no, it fell a dead weight upon the ears of all." The inference is that both Wordsworth's printed pamphlets and his word of mouth had previously fallen dead on the mind of the electorate. The two papers are a perfect pattern of what a campaign document ought not to be.

One wonders, in pondering the question of Wordsworth's greatness as a political poet how far he consciously modeled himself on Milton. He hoped to do for his own day what Milton had done for the England of an earlier day. He won his sure place in the poetic succession; it is much less certain that he was Milton's peer and heir in realms of state. A determination to wear the whole of his predecessor's toga may have led him to place in his powers of political thought a confidence which they did not deserve. Wordsworth's political tracts ought to be compared closely with Milton's, to discover whether there is not in them a deliberate imitation of Milton's manner and even of his vocabulary. Such a comparison might yield no positive result, but, even were this to be so, the suspicion remains that Wordsworth the political poet was never spontaneous or natural, because he had Milton too much in mind to be himself. Wordsworth felt that, for England's good, Milton ought to be living at that hour; but since this was a vain fancy, he did his best to play Milton to the later day, and precisely because he was playing a rôle he never made personal connection with the events he hoped to guide. If there be any ground for these suspicions, they would be wholly in keeping with all else that we know of Wordsworth's mental habits, a too great dependence at such points upon the minds of others.

What then remains of Wordsworth's claim to a place among the political poets? How far was he, in his own right, a politically-minded man? The answer is reasonably clear, and within its limits satisfactory. Wordsworth believed in the kind of human life he had first envisaged in the Lake Country. His vision of man and a consequent love of man had come tardily,[1] but like all things of slow growth, they were strong. The scene of his Utopia was always some narrow vale where "each is known to all." The shield of human nature disclosed there should be approached from the golden side. The story of Michael, he tells us, was the first of those domestic tales that discovered man to him as the crown of nature, in the person of the overruling shepherd:

> An old man, stout of heart, and strong of limb.
> His bodily frame had been from youth to age
> Of an unusual strength: his mind was keen,
> Intense, and frugal, apt for all affairs.
>   . . . he had been alone
> Amid the heart of many thousand mists.

Wordsworth's subsequent heroes were permutations and combinations of the virtues incarnate in Michael. The Wanderer is the same man under another name:

> And every moral feeling of his soul
> Strengthened and braced, by breathing in content
> The keen, the wholesome, air of poverty,
> And drinking from the well of homely life.

The eighth book of *The Prelude* gives us the poet's fullest elaboration of his political ideal:

> Man free, man working for himself, with choice
> Of time, and place, and object. . . .
> And suffering among awful Powers and Forms.

> What need to follow him through what he does
> Or sees in his day's march. He feels himself
> A Freeman; wedded to his life of hope
> And hazard, and hard labour interchang'd
> With that majestic indolence so dear
> To native Man. . . .

---

1. In *The Prelude*, VIII, he says that until he was twenty-three, man was in his affections and regards subordinate to nature.

... blessed be the God
Of Nature and of Man. ...
That Men did at the first present themselves
Before my untaught eyes thus purified,
Remov'd, and at a distance that was fit.

The Human nature unto which I felt
That I belong'd, and which I lov'd and reverenc'd,
Was not a punctual Presence, but a Spirit
Living in time and space, and far diffus'd.

One remembers Lincoln's words about the Union; what he did about slavery and what he left undone were conditioned by his desire to save the Union. Wordsworth might have said the same of the changes of political opinion with which he is charged. His one desire was to insure to the world men like Michael. He was a revolutionist as long as the Revolution promised to yield him such men. When the Revolution failed him here, degenerating into a new tyranny, he lost all interest in it. He turned to Toryism because political thinking of that type seemed to him at the time more likely than any other to guarantee him his freeman. Like many another statesman Wordsworth was a frank opportunist in pursuit of his political ideals.

Wordsworth's sympathy with the French Revolution was therefore never an independent or a primary matter. It was the corollary of a prior loyalty, his faith in the sort of persons whom he later made his chosen heroes. He could put off his revolutionary ideas without any sense of treason, because he had put them on without serious reflection. At this point Legouis, and all who have followed his lead, have misread the poet. William Wordsworth was from first to last a stubborn north-country Englishman, anxious above all else, in political matters, to perpetuate the society in which he had grown up as a boy and youth. He concluded, as affairs went their way from the Terror through Waterloo, that the English Constitution was more certain to give him his ideal than were the illusory French Rights of Man. Who shall say that he was wrong?

There is no doubt that Wordsworth's freeman was in large part a creation of his own imagination. There is far more in Wordsworth's *Michael* than its original can ever have suspected of himself. It could not have been otherwise, since Wordsworth was writing poetry and not a poor-law report. Nevertheless, Harriet Martineau once burst out about the legendary figure who was Wordsworth's political hero:

> I, deaf, can hardly conceive how he with eyes & ears & a heart which leads him to converse with the poor in his incessant walks can be so unaware of their social state. I dare say y° need not be told how sensual vice abounds in rural districts. Here it is flagrant beyond anything I ever co[d] have looked for & here while every justice of the peace is filled with disgust & every clergyman with almost despair at the drunkenness quarrells & extreme licentiousness with women — here is dear good old W. for ever talk[g] of rural innocence & deprecat[g] any intercourse with the towns lest the purity of his neighbours sho[d] be corrupted.

Miss Martineau was much nearer the facts than Wordsworth was. That is beside the mark. Wordsworth continued to look on the golden side of the human shield and would have agreed that in his treatment of man, as in his treatment of nature, he only half found his poem in the original subject and in equal half created it by imagination. The one thing to remember in our discussion of Wordsworth's political thinking is this: he believed in the freeman whom he had first seen and then had idealized in the narrow valleys of his childhood, and he was willing to identify himself with any school of political thought which promised the perpetuation of the type and fuller realization of the ideal. Should the wheel ever come full circle, and England be again what she was once, an agricultural community with a population only a fraction of its present numbers — and both Stanley Baldwin and Dean Inge have prophesied this destiny for England within a century or so — then Wordsworth's political thinking may again become plausible and even far-sighted. The world has known few men nobler than Michael.

In 1844 Horne set this whole question of Wordsworth as a radical or a reactionary in something like a true perspective:

After twenty years of public abuse and laughter, William Wordsworth is now regarded by the public of the country as the prophet of his age. And this is not a right view — after all. . . . He does not cry aloud to mankind like "a voice in the wilderness," that the way should be "made straight," that a golden age will come, or a better age, or that the time may come when "poor humanity's afflicted will" shall *not* struggle altogether in vain with ruthless destiny. His Sonnets in favour of the punishment of Death, chiefly on the ground of not venturing to meddle with an old law, are the tomb of his prophet-title. He is a prophet of the Past. His futurity is in the eternal form of things, and the aspiration of his soul towards the spirit of the universe; but as for the destinies of mankind, he looks back upon them with a sigh, and thinks that, as they were in the beginning, so shall they be world without end. His "future can but be the past." He dictates, he does not predict: he is a teacher and a preacher in the highest sense, but he does not image forth the To-Come, nor sound the trumpet of mighty changes in the horizon.[1]

Meanwhile, it is a mistaken view of Wordsworth which would have us believe that he ever became Tory in personal manners. He was to the last an uncorrupted democrat. In a letter to Henry Reed (1845) the poet describes his presentation at Court. Self-pity has seldom mixed the comic and the grave so nicely:

1. R. H. Horne, *The New Spirit of the Age* (New York: Harper and Brothers, 1844), p. 177.

The reception given me by the young Queen at her Ball was most gracious. Mrs. Everett the wife of your minister among others was a witness to it; without knowing who I was. It moved her to the shedding of tears. The effect was in part produced, I suppose by the American habits of feeling, as pertaining to a republican government like yours. To see a grey haired Man 75 years of age kneeling down in a large assembly, to kiss the hand of a young woman is a sight for which institutions essentially democratic do not prepare a spectator of either sex, and must naturally place the opinions upon which a Republic is founded, and the sentiments which support it, in strong contrast with a government based & upheld as ours is.

The poet intimates that he thought Mrs. Everett's tears fully warranted.

The history, thus reconstructed, fails to confirm the critical convention that Wordsworth's poetic decline was due to a change of political opinions.

CHAPTER VI

Annette

WHEN Wordsworth died in 1850 *The Times*, in its obituary notice, dwelt on the example of his blameless life, "as pure and spotless as his song." The poets, it goes on to say, spread moral infection wider than other men, because those brought within their influence are singularly susceptible of contamination. In this respect Wordsworth's fellow-craftsmen in the first years of the century had not been free from blame. The Victorian age took comfort in remembering that, whatever might have been true of Byron and Shelley, neither by his writing nor by his example had Wordsworth "corrupted or ennervated our youth."

He had been the single-minded and rather unexciting husband of one wife, whose loyalty and respect were supposedly his letters-patent of purity. His contemporaries thought of him as "a good sturdy Tory, a most exemplary man in all the relations of life, and a stamp-master void of reproach." [1] They were particularly impressed by "the purity — the domestic purity we may call it — of Wordsworth's descriptions of woman." [2] He passed into English letters, in 1850, as the least likely subject of his day for eventual indictment as a lawless lover. As late as 1909 Professor Bradley was still commenting in the traditional vein upon Wordsworth's "grave . . . and moral treatment of sexual passion."

1. *Fraser's Magazine*, VI (1832), 313.
2. *The Dublin University Magazine*, XXXVI (1850), 336.

The disinterment of Annette has changed the picture. Wordsworth has now become a lost leader in this other ancient and most uncertain of all human causes. The discovery of the early liaison has been variously received. Wordsworth's rather tedious goodness had long irritated the philistines, who now have full warrant for unholy mirth at the story of the French mistress and the illegitimate daughter. The poet's idolaters were thrown into consternation and found themselves hard put to it to cover his nakedness with the shreds of his reputation for the proprieties. But now that the laughter has died down and the tears are dried, we find in the incident one of the pass-keys to the poet's history as a man and an artist. Without this tale, we are to gather, the works remain a misleading clue to their author's true character and a sealed mystery of themselves.

Looking back, the wonder is that the secret was kept. It is to the poet's credit that he never hid the truth from his near of kin and his friends; those who were entitled to know the story heard it. Dorothy, Mary, and presumably Coleridge, were the first to be told. In due time Francis Wrangham, the Clarksons, the Montagus, Crabb Robinson, Quillinan, and Miss Fenwick were also initiated into the conspiracy of silence. At the very least ten or a dozen persons were in possession of the disquieting facts.[1] Given our human tendency to betray confidences, it says much for the loyalty of Wordsworth's friends that the affair did not become a matter of common talk. He must have persuaded all concerned that he had acted honorably, and that nothing was to be gained by giving the story to the world.

Now that the dust of the discovery has begun to settle we can see that our one serious interest in the affair with

1. The most recent criticism of Wordsworth asserts that during all his mature life Wordsworth was harassed by a sense of guilt over the Annette affair. As I understand the new psychology a "guilt feeling" requires, as its premise, secrecy. Wordsworth told at least a dozen persons about Annette, and can hardly be charged with concealing a guilty secret.

Annette is its reaction on the poet. The woman herself does not greatly stir our sympathy. She was, in 1792, four or five years older than Wordsworth, and the difference in years added to what would have been her greater maturity had they been of an age. As Professor Legouis and Professor Harper have recovered her for us, Annette is sentimental and sententious. She plays very skilfully upon Wordsworth's compassion in the one or two letters, still extant, which she sent after him to England. Perhaps we are ungenerous to her in saying that she found some consolation in her rôle as a tragedy queen, but she was not wanting in a woman's wiles and her appeal to her lover is shrewdly calculated. If the deserted mothers of whom Wordsworth later wrote — supposedly in great contrition — were copied from Annette, we can only say that the poet did not write with his eye fixed steadily on his model. They depart very far from the French woman with her pretty affectations and her torrent of protestations.

In due time the daughter Caroline and her husband Badouin became the heirs of the grievance. In 1850 Wordsworth's literary executors found themselves liable to what was little less than blackmail. One would have thought that by constant payments and a generous settlement Wordsworth would have earned their silence.[1] We cannot pretend to be greatly stirred by the calculated information sent to England sixty years after the "love-likings" on the Loire that now "the granddaughter is in distress." Christopher Wordsworth was faced with the prospect that the Badouins would print the whole story, and there were anxious moments at home. He was afraid that "the French people will try to get money from the family as the price of silence, & failing in that, they will make up and publish a revelation which will be as romantic as French ingenuity can make it." There is here a

---

1. For twenty years from 1815 Wordsworth had given Caroline an annual allowance of £30, and in 1835 had made a final settlement of £400.

healthy Anglo-Saxon respect for the traditional Gallic skill in eroticism. Eventually the oil of Crabb Robinson's diplomacy seems to have quieted the Badouins. We can only assume that they were, in so many words, bought off. The nephew was able in the biography to negotiate the incident by an elision, but his silence on the subject must have given thereafter added substance to his episcopal petition for forgiveness for things left undone. In retrospect, however, Badouin and his wife are not seen as admirable or pleasant persons. There is altogether too much suggestion of the refined scrupulousness in money matters which has been one of the dubious distinctions of bourgeois France. If, by 1850, we must take sides, we prefer the impulsive Wordsworth of 1792 to the calculating French family of 1850.

As for the affair itself, all the extenuating circumstances have been duly noted and entered by Professors Legouis and Harper. We are reminded that eighteenth-century English standards in such matters, particularly in the North, were not over-exacting; that in France Wordsworth was without the ordinary restraints provided by home; that he may well have tried to marry Annette at the time and failed to do so because Catholic marriage — the only marriage to which she would have consented — was not recognized by the state; that her royalist sympathies put her beyond the processes of civil marriage; that the poet went back to England hoping to make money to support himself, his mistress, and his child; and that he fully intended to come back and marry her, but was prevented from doing so by the declaration of war. Altogether nature is not to be wholly condemned if in the face of such difficulties she took her own way. We do not stop twice to explain like happenings in the lives of other poets; we linger over this one merely because it involved that improbable person, William Wordsworth.

Nor has anyone ever suggested that Wordsworth should

have nurtured his affection during a long enforced separation from the end of 1792 until the Peace of Amiens in 1803 and gone back to France to make Annette his lawful wife. Again, there was at work a strong persuasion which convinced him, with the passage of the years, that Annette was not "made for him." There are no tears to be spilt that Wordsworth failed to make Mlle. Vallon an honest woman. The thing is unthinkable. Wordsworth would have been preposterous as a citizen of France, a clerk in some provincial French city; and Annette would have been *déracinée* and miserable in the Lake District. The passion of the body could not have prevailed permanently over the discrepancy of temperament and interest.

Let it be said at once that the story has rescued Wordsworth from a world of bleak correctness to which his own silence and his growing reputation had condemned him, and has planted him once more among fallible human beings. We are a little more at ease in his company than once we were. "We never think," says a reviewer in 1816, "of claiming kindred with Mr. Wordsworth as a man of the same nerve and texture of heart's blood with ourselves." The critics noted from the first his avoidance of romantic love as a theme for verse. The absence of the subject was put down to his nature or taste; he was supposed to be constitutionally incapable of sensuous love, or temperamentally disinterested in it. His marriage to Mary Hutchinson did not suggest ardor, and Crabb Robinson once reminded him that he had gone out of his way to assure the world that he had not married her for her beauty. In general he was reported "never to have passed through an erotic period" and his verse was said to be wanting in "dark moral recesses." De Quincey in a shrewd passage came nearer the truth than he knew: "Yet, if no lover, or (which some of us have sometimes thought) a lover disappointed at some earlier period by the death of her he loved, or by some other fatal accident." At a much later time Leslie Stephen would not have been surprised and would have understood. And now, once the first surprise has passed, we also understand, and understanding do not condemn.

Our one permanent interest in the whole episode, then, is its effect on the man. If he felt "a guilty thing" whenever he remembered his defection from republicanism, did he feel doubly guilty when he thought of his desertion of Annette? If so, did this guilt impair his integrity to such an extent that he was denied thereafter the unity of spirit which art requires? Is the poetry of the golden decade already vitiated by a guilt-feeling, and was his dreary anti-climax the hollow triumph of that feeling over the single-minded man he might have been? These are the questions which concern the critic today.

We have said that the present period of Wordsworth criticism began with Professor Legouis' study of the poet's youth, published in 1896. The period must be drawing to its conclusion with two books published within the last four or five years, Mr. Herbert Read's *Wordsworth* and Mr. Hugh I'Anson Fausset's *The Lost Leader*. It is difficult to see how the general principle of criticism initiated by Legouis can be carried further. Wordsworth's French amour is now found to have been his sentence of poetic death. Both of the books assume that the inconclusive affair with Annette destroyed the poet's integrity as a man and from the outset impaired his art. The detailed arguments need not be reviewed here; an intimation of their general trend will suffice.

Mr. Read's case may be abridged in his own words:

I think that this passion and all its melancholy aftermath was the deepest experience of Wordsworth's life — the emotional complex from which all his subsequent career flows in its intricacy and uncertainty. It was this experience which Wordsworth saw fit to hide — to bury in a most complete secrecy and mask with a long sustained hypocrisy. . . .

Why pry into the matter at all? it may be asked. I have already answered that question. Wordsworth, as a character and as a poet, is inexplicable without this key to his emotional development. With this key he becomes, not indeed, a rational being, but a man whose thwarted emotions found an external and objective compensation in his poetry. . . .

There is a saying of Richepin's to the effect that the love of art involves the loss of real love. Wordsworth's change of nature during these years illustrates its profound truth. As the love for Annette grew less, another change took place. We never suddenly lose an emotional attachment; we slowly bury it under rational camouflage. And so from now onwards we find Wordsworth losing faith in France, losing faith in those humanitarian ideals for which France was a symbol. Why? Because he was transferring to France the effects of his cooling affection for Annette. He could not avow to himself his loss of love for Annette; but he could give his uneasy conscience scope in the idea of the country and nation to which she belonged. Wordsworth was recovering his stability, finding his ideal self or personality, his philosophy of nature and his poetic genius; he was losing Annette, his faith in youth and change, his fundamental honesty.[1]

Mr. Fausset's indictment is more leisurely and diffuse, but none the less drastic:

For the first and last time in his life he was completely possessed by love for a woman. The inmost defences of his selfhood went down before the rapture that seized him. He was blindly infatuated as only those who have jealously and austerely guarded the shrine of their being can be, when life compels them to fling open the doors.

This passion which possessed him so feverishly was in truth a fallacious spring, and snatching too hastily at its blossom, he precluded love from ever coming to true fruition in his experience.

In France he had lost his integrity and entered the path of compromise. Deep down within him he felt that he had been

---

1. Herbert Read, *Wordsworth* (London: Jonathan Cape, 1930), pp. 96, 97, 134.

false to his truer and purer being. If he could have candidly
faced the fact and humbled himself before it, he might have ex-
pelled its poison from his blood. But although inwardly humili-
ated, he was not humbled. And so the furies of perplexity,
shame, and remorse were already on his track. Through the
next few years they were to infest his nights and days. And by
resisting and suppressing them he was to strengthen the defensive egoism which had saved him indeed from returning with
the Brissotins 'to the breast of Nature,'

> With all my resolutions, all my hopes,
> A poet only to myself, to men
> Useless,

but which was to curtail sadly his development both as a poet
and a man.

He failed, and lived for forty years haunted by an uneasy
conscience, a sense of faded glory, of vision darkened, and deep
assurance quenched.

Wordsworth was to spend his life in a self-defensive warfare,
culminating in barren self-righteousness. . . . In the *Lines Left
upon a Seat in a Yew-tree* we have the first hint of the false compromise which he was to accept, of the self-deception of the
moralist who preaches humility without having really humbled
himself. And this recoil from the ultimate demands of life behind the defences of a lofty morality necessitated also that he
should henceforth shrink with something of a morbid horror
from those physical desires which had become associated in his
mind with his fall into sin. To contemplate them not only hurt
his conscience; it injured the self esteem which he wished to re-
establish. And this revulsion crippled eventually both his instinctive and his rational being. It made it impossible for him
really to recover his sense of the innocence of life, and by poison-
ing for him the deepest of the natural channels of life, it led ultimately to spiritual impotence.

Wordsworth was a poetical mystic who failed to complete
himself at a crucial point. . . . All his natural faculties which in
his short inspired period had been channels for a life and consciousness which transcended the narrow bounds of self, lost
touch with their spiritual source and came to serve beneath a

mask of piety, morality, and high principles, the barren needs of a nervous egoism.[1]

On either score, Mr. Read's or Mr. Fausset's, we have an explanation of Wordsworth's decline as an artist. Annette was the source of his undoing. We need seek no further for any account of his waning poetical powers. His integrity being forfeit, he was prohibited from writing great poetry, once the inner malady reached the surface of his conscious art.

Mr. Read implies that Wordsworth was not aware of the way in which his defense mechanisms operated; the process went on in the unconscious areas of the mind. He was able, therefore, to write for ten years great poetry, being ignorant of his mortal ill. Mr. Fausset, on the other hand, suggests that Wordsworth was fully aware of his moral and spiritual extremity, and that his acts of self-deception were willed. The poet is, therefore, more culpable on the latter count than on the former. Fausset agrees that the experience of Tintern revisited in 1798, which yielded us one of the greatest of Wordsworth's poems, was in his life as an artist the most profound which he ever had; "he could believe that he had come through the shadow into mellow sunlight." But the carefully qualified reference to this belief suggests that it was not a faith warranted by the facts. *Tintern Abbey* is, to Mr. Fausset, the product of Wordsworth's desperate will to believe in his integrity, and the desperateness of the attempt is betrayed by a strain felt in the poem.

These two books are the most serious indictment of Wordsworth which criticism has yet achieved. They are on the whole sympathetic rather than savage; they lack the vitriol in which Jeffrey dipped his pen, but their pity is even more devastating than the reckless blame of a cen-

1. Hugh I'Anson Fausset, *The Lost Leader* (New York: Harcourt, Brace and Company, 1933), pp. 103, 105, 117–118, 9, 171–172, 8. By permission of Harcourt, Brace and Company.

tury gone. We are no longer dealing with differences of opinion about poetic diction, principles of esthetics, choice of subjects; we are confronted with an indictment of the man which involves the artist. Should this most recent opinion prevail and such analyses of the poet become the critical convention of the future, the last vestiges of the traditional Wordsworth will have disappeared. The logic lying between Professor Legouis' book, published in 1896, and these latest studies has been consecutive and perhaps consistent. Its major premise is the assumption that the truth of Wordsworth is to be sought in the light of the two or three agonized years from 1792 to 1795. All that followed them was a mental and emotional consequence, compensation, imperfect readjustment. Annette Vallon is the apex of an inverted pyramid, and must account for the whole unstable mass of nearly sixty years of poetic insincerity.

The weight which we give to such a reconstruction of Wordsworth's history will depend in part upon the importance which we attach to the newer psychology and in greater part upon our estimate of the man. Let it be said at once that Wordsworth was bound to fall into the hands of the modern psychoanalytic biographer. No exemptions are promised to any heroic figure in the past, and given the opportune discovery of Annette, Wordsworth could not hope to escape.

Mr. Read makes use of the familiar theories of transference in accounting for Wordsworth's eventual distaste for France. Being at the first unable to marry Annette, concluding after a time that he no longer wished to marry Annette, his love for her changing into a positive distaste, Wordsworth shifts his disaffection and objectifies in his repudiation of the Revolution his desertion of the mistress. His antipathy to France is thus an unconscious mounting hatred of the woman he has ceased to love.

We cannot deny that such transferences and compensations take place in life. They seem to be proved beyond all question of a doubt and to account for otherwise inexplicable emotions. But this method of explaining our mysterious antipathies is invoked only when a more obvious explanation is wanting. It is a fair question whether we need to employ any such complicated apparatus to account for Wordsworth's recoil from the course of the French Revolution. Had there been no Annette we cannot conceive, knowing Wordsworth as we do, that his attitude toward France would have been different. He might have been spared, or might have shortened, the Godwin interlude, which had a very intimate bearing upon his state of mind and heart just after 1793. But none of the known facts suggests that Wordsworth would have remained loyal to the Revolution, would have yielded up his life as a forlorn and fruitless victim of the guillotine, or would have languished in jail with his fellow-English Jacobins. Dorothy says with disarming candor that William was "prudent" in these matters. Meanwhile his disaffection with the Revolution can be accounted for on its own terms. True, Annette, France, the Revolution, his frustrated love, all made up a complex state of mind and heart in the life of a single man, but the theory that without Annette Wordsworth's change of political opinion is unintelligible — if there was a change — is over-subtle. The Revolution was breeding tyrants and martyrs, not freemen wedded to a life of hope and love; that was why Wordsworth repudiated it in its later stages. The coincidence in time of the Annette affair with this other history need not mean their interdependence or identification.

Mr. Fausset's study is written in sorrow rather than in dispassionateness; he both explains and blames. He indicts Wordsworth, as a belated Moses, for forfeiting the moral right to enter a Promised Land which was opening before him, — the nineteenth century with its milk and honey of romanticism. Wordsworth, he tells us, failed as a survival of the eighteenth century to negotiate the spiritual traverse

between that time and the age which ensued. Indeed, in
his fatal slip he carried down with him many followers who
were roped to the precedent he set. At its very inception
he condemned nineteenth-century romanticism to futility,
since in Wordsworth's sin we sinned all.

Wordsworth's guilt was this, that he was not willing to
admit to himself that he had sinned. He never humbled
himself before his accusing conscience, but built up a
stony defense of self-righteousness, so that "the guilty
thing" he really was should never "surprise" him or catch
him off his guard. Mr. Fausset, using evangelical language, does not imply that Wordsworth had sinned with
Annette, but that he thought he had sinned and would not
admit it — a far graver matter. His sin was not the act of
the flesh, — that could be understood and condoned, — it
was his subsequent Pharisaism. Had he once trusted his
wounded nature and cried out for mercy, everything might
have been well.

Such an inference depends upon our estimate of the sort
of man William Wordsworth was. Personally, I find it difficult to follow its logic because again — as in the case of
the theory that an unbroken friendship with Coleridge
would have yielded great verse for an indefinite period —
it calls for a man whom we do not find elsewhere in the
sources. The argument imputes to Wordsworth a romantic temperament, to say nothing of an evangelical religion,
which he wholly lacked.

Not that Wordsworth was a stranger to the life of the
body and its primal thrusts. The drawing of him by Han-
cock, made in 1798, now in the National Portrait Gallery,
shows lips which are thick, sensual, and even brutal; eyes
which are smouldering; and a face suggesting forthright
passion. We can readily believe that the senses of such a
man could be stung into swift and imperious action. The
face is not that of an ascetic. On the other hand, it is not
the face of a sentimental lover, for it lacks subtlety and

any suggestion of romantic sensitiveness. The picture
bears out De Quincey's statement that as a young man
Wordsworth showed "preternatural animal sensibility"
in all the primal passions.

We take it for granted that, aside from Mary Hutchinson, Annette Vallon was the only woman whom Wordsworth had ever "known." By what right do we do so?
The argument from silence proves nothing, and once our
minds have become adjusted to the mistress in the picture,
as well as to the wife, we are not required to suppose that
Wordsworth first met Venus in the arms of Annette. Mr.
Garrod hints quite plainly that he regards the assumption
as gratuitous. He calls our attention to the poet's candid
references to "the frank-hearted maids of Cumberland,"
to "shocks of young love-liking," to "nights of revelry"
in the company of these same maids, and bids us draw our
own inferences.

Wordsworth, in his later years, lived almost solely in the
company of women. He was reproached by the world for
barricading himself so effectually behind skirts. But the
picture of these years is not one of a philanderer, rather it is
that of a male creature who has become dependent upon
one woman, or many, to smooth his way through the day's
affairs. Wordsworth may have relied over-much upon his
housekeepers to make him comfortable, but he was not
emotionally the master of a harem.

The woman who entered most deeply into his life was
his sister. Both Mr. Read and Mr. Fausset skirt this
subject with discreet periphrasis. The former does not
suggest that there was "anything sinister in Dorothy's
affection for her brother." But, having raised the ghost,
he cannot lay it. The relation between William and
Dorothy "had in it an element of romantic love ... neither
consciously recognized the fact, but unconsciously they
betrayed it." In short, there was in their mutual affection
the stuff of incest. We are told that this emotional compli-

cation was the result of the transference to the recovered sister of all the thwarted feelings which had been dissociated from the lost mistress. I doubt such a psychology; the roots of an incestuous relationship between brother and sister normally go back either to childhood or to infancy. But whatever the explanation may be, all other women, Annette included, stood once removed in Wordsworth's life from his tender passion for Dorothy.[1] Without the aid of our modern apparatus for knowing ourselves, the two were happily spared an understanding of the implications of their affection and are blameless in their feelings as in their action. In critical retrospect we may make what we will, psychologically, of the facts, yet their patent truth denies to Annette the power to pull open the doors to the shrine of Wordsworth's being. And how un-Wordsworthian the metaphor is!

It is hard to resist the conclusion that Wordsworth was constitutionally disinterested in things erotic. Not that he was not capable of passion as a man. No man utterly insensible to love could have written the line,

> Soft bosoms breathe around contagious sighs.

Not only so, he had gone further, and had tasted the lover's sweet distraction:

> The house she dwelt in was a sainted shrine,
> Her chamber-window did surpass in glory
> The portals of the East: all paradise
> Could by the simple opening of a door
> Let itself in upon him.

---

1. Dorothy's language in describing their intimacy is stronger than her brother's: "We made a pillow of my shoulder . . . and my beloved slept." As for the theory that Dorothy was the victim of an unrequited and forbidden love for Coleridge, Mr. de Selincourt, in *Dorothy Wordsworth* (Oxford: Clarendon Press, 1933), p. 132, wisely says, "her passion for her brother was so intense as to preclude her from feeling for any other man an emotion which would have satisfied the physical as well as the spiritual side of her nature."

Here is love poetry, and very great love poetry. It was
emotion recollected in tranquillity — his own story on the
Loire, disguised as the tale of *Vaudracour and Julia*. But
when you have cited these two passages and the mentions
of the "frank-hearted maids" of Cumberland or Italy you
have exhausted the love poems of William Wordsworth in
the conventional sense of that term.

We do not forget that in the *Lucy* lines he wrote greater
love poetry than this, of a power and penetration not
matched in stray mentions of "love-likings." We do not
know who Lucy was, whether an ideal, a memory, or a
compound of many women; but, whoever she was, Wordsworth loved her deeply, though his lines to her are un-
troubled by "contagious sighs." We are not dealing here
with a woman of flesh and blood. If her image haunted
the poet, she came to quiet rather than to vex him. She
stands apart from all experiences of either ecstasy or guilt,
and the recollection of her is tranquil.

Wordsworth seems thus to have been a man capable of
passion, and Annette tasted his passion. Yet there is
nothing in any of the sources to indicate that such passion
was the first truth of the man or the scene of his central
concern. Mary Hutchinson won and kept his affection,
but presumably without the passion. Annette may have
had the passion, though she never wakened the affection.
The strange relationship with Dorothy was of a different
kind, obscure in its beginnings, and never fully conscious
of itself, much less of its nature. Finally there was the
Lucy of his imagination, a woman whom he created rather
than found.

First-hand impressions are more important than second-
hand inferences. Coleridge once opened his mind to Crabb
Robinson on Wordsworth as a lover:

Thus, Wordsworth is by nature incapable of being in Love,
tho' no man more tenderly attached — hence he ridicules the

existence of any other passion, than a compound of Lust with
Esteem and Friendship, confined to one Object, first by accidents of association, and permanently by the force of Habit and
a sense of Duty. Now this will do very well — it will suffice to
make a good Husband — it may even be desirable (if the largest
sum of easy and pleasurable sensations in this Life be the right
aim and end of human Wisdom) that we should have this, and
no more — but still it is not Love.[1]

Nothing that has ever been said of Wordsworth's capac-
ity for love is as consonant with all else we know of him.
Coleridge's words put Wordsworth entirely out of bounds
as the irregular hero of a romantic love affair and therefore
as a victim of subsequent guilt-feelings.

Byron — who had no little erotic experience — says that
"man's love is of man's life a thing apart." William
Wordsworth seems to have been just such a man as a lover,
whether of Dorothy, or Annette, or Mary. There was a
core of hard self-sufficiency which none of the three women
— not even his sister — ever touched. His independence
was a limitation of his nature and may have been a defect
in his character. It made him a selfish man, for of his inordinately self-centered life there is abundant proof. But
the doors to the shrine of his being were never flung wide
to any human being whatsoever; they were fully open
only toward the natural world.

The psychoanalytic critics will say that the affair with
Annette froze up the poet's human-heartedness and made
him thereafter afraid of simple and direct emotions. They
are under bonds, however, to produce for us prior to 1792
a youth likely to have matured directly in warm and genial
affections, had not his heart suffered the rebuke of his conscience. True, the sources for positing this or any other
kind of youth are meager, and want of evidence may allow
such a reconstruction. Nevertheless, the dominant im-

---

1. Earl Leslie Griggs, *Unpublished Letters of Samuel Taylor Coleridge* (London: Constable and Company, 1932), II, 46.

pression we have of Wordsworth is that of a man capable of "animal sensibility," but much too preoccupied with himself to allow the selflessness required to make good a romantic account of his supposedly devastating love for Annette.

All recent critics point to the prominence in Wordsworth's verse of the "deserted mother" theme, and are agreed that in his repeated treatment of the subject the poet found emotional relief and perhaps some measure of escape from the burden of his guilt. Patently the objectification of such experiences in art provides release, and the process is not merely a recognized one, it is also highly recommended. Had Wordsworth been able to consult a psychiatrist in his extremity the course which he is said to have followed would have been the one professionally proposed to him. Meanwhile the frequency of the theme is supposed to be a proof of the deep-seated nature of the moral disease.

On the other hand the citation of these "deserted mother" poems presses the autobiographical reference to the extreme. We are entitled to at least an occasional reservation before we accept the argument. Wordsworth insisted that the tale of *Vaudracour and Julia* had independent warrant, and Mr. de Selincourt sees no reason to doubt his statement, even though he may have intended Coleridge, to whom *The Prelude* was dedicated, to draw his own conclusions about its autobiographical pertinence in the original setting. Moreover we need to remember that Wordsworth's themes, so far as his human subjects are concerned, were few and their permutations and combinations limited. In the main, his poems deal with sadness rather than with gayety, and if he turned to the immemorial lot of woman for a subject, the deserted mother was the one always nearest to his hand, his own history quite apart. It is not as though William Wordsworth had discovered the deserted mother or had created her out of nothing. She is a commonplace in art.

Running through all the poems which find their subject in gray-cloaked figures on the lonely horizons of the Wordsworth scene there is the constant suggestion of human beings bereft of those nearest and most necessary to them. Conceivably Wordsworth's own orphaned childhood, the homeless lot of his early years, and the uncertain welcome he had from kinsmen may have planted in his mind the germs of the idea of human desolateness. For Wordsworth always dwells on life's absences rather than its presences. Michael is in the terms of a man's life the equivalent of Margaret. When we press this bereftness, to see wherein it consists, we usually find that it is the broken link between father and son or mother and child, rather than between the man and the woman.

If the affair with Annette left a scar on Wordsworth's heart and conscience, the scar was not made by Annette herself, but by Annette *and* Caroline and ultimately by the daughter rather than the mother.[1] Had there been no child it is doubtful whether Wordsworth would have been seriously affected by the liaison. It was probably the coming of the child, the fact of the illegitimate daughter, which gave him what actual unease he had. The forthright traditions of a country district have always required that under such circumstances the man shall make the woman "honest," and all we know of the event suggests that for an indefinite time after 1792 Wordsworth intended to do so. Indeed, in leaving Annette shortly before the child was born, to make his way to England in search of money, he intimates that he was more concerned for her equivocal status than in love with herself. There is about his parting from her just at that time precisely the insensibility of which we have ample evidence at a later date. The incident runs true to all we know of the Wordsworth form:

1. Sara Coleridge to H. C. R., June 29, 1843: "While Mr. Wordsworth's poems abound in pictures of human sorrow of the deepest pathos . . . by far the greatest number of them relate to the loss of children."

prudence, foresight, a rather chilly rectitude, but certainly not love as the romantics exemplify it. As with France, so with Annette, — "not mine, and such as was not made for me."

Back in England the poet had no wish to shirk the obligations incurred by the indulgence of his passion. There is every reason to believe that he made one desperate trip to France in 1793 but failed to reach Annette, having been turned back by the state of affairs in Paris. Had he persisted he would probably have lost his life. Nine years later the diaries make frequent mention of "A." In the spring months of 1802 just before his marriage to Mary Hutchinson Wordsworth was in a nervous and overwrought state. The repeated references to letters from France suggest that he was trying to bring his relation to Annette to something like a decent conclusion before his wedding. But the whole connotation of these references, as of the trip to Calais and the meeting with Annette and Caroline, is that of prudence rather than of a reawakened love or of a guilt that would not down. As a human being Wordsworth is at this point perhaps a less admirable man than we could wish, yet such is the inference to be drawn from the facts which we have, unless we approach the sources determined in advance to make them yield to the psychoanalytic reconstruction.

We might conceivably consent to the guilt hypothesis were it not for one preposterous incident which refuses to be included in any such scheme. In the summer of 1820 William, Mary, Dorothy, Crabb Robinson, the Monkhouses, and Miss Horrocks went on a tour of the Continent. October found them in Paris, and they spent the entire month on the Rue Charlot, where Annette, Caroline, and her husband were living. There was much friendly visiting back and forth. I, for one, find it impossible to believe that the will to self-righteousness is capable of such a superhuman victory over a guilty conscience. Given a sense of sin resolutely crushed by a studied hypocrisy, it is inconceivable that even twenty-five years after the initial agony the poet would have risked reopening the old wound. William Wordsworth could expose his wife, his sister, and his friends to the awkwardness of such meetings only because he had no personal feeling about them, and was void of all delicacy of perception. The solemn pilgrimages along the Rue Charlot were prompted by insensibility rather than self-righteousness.

Annette, then, was the partner of an experience which on Wordsworth's side undoubtedly engaged his passion and mitigated his loneliness in a strange land; we may even concede a genuine camaraderie. As a mistress she brought him pleasure. She became a problem when she became a mother. What to do about her, for her, puzzled the scrupulous Wordsworth for years thereafter. We make her chargeable for more than is her share if we find in her the source of a poison which was to infect his earliest verse and finally to paralyze his matured genius. Wordsworth, even in Blois and Orleans, had a life quite apart from Annette. Intellectually and emotionally he was a celibate nature; he fulfils the requirements of that line of Ibsen's, "You are a company of bachelors, you don't see a woman." Only on some such hypothesis does his history explain itself.

On the guilt theory we are required to believe that for eight or ten years, beginning with the *Lyrical Ballads*, Wordsworth achieved a superhuman feat of moral self-deception. The poems of the golden decade, while they have their peculiarities and perhaps their limitations, are intense and unified as little poetry is. On their face they do not seem to be a succession of shrewd sins against the Holy Ghost. I find it impossible to believe that *Tintern Abbey* is the work of a consciously guilty man, who by some sophistry has persuaded himself that he is righteous. So radically vicious an act must betray itself in the text. I can understand that a critic might read such a history into

the poem; I fail to see how, wanting the initial psychoanalytic hypotheses, he could read it out of the poem as it
stands. If *Tintern Abbey* harbors the lie in the soul, that
fact should betray itself through internal evidence. So, if
the *Lyrical Ballads* in their entirety are not the work of a
genuinely integrated character, of a man who has brought
order out of chaos in his own life, then none of our judgments in such matters are to be trusted, and we must take
refuge in the humiliating reflection that any knave can
dupe us.

The source of Wordsworth's dismal anti-climax may not
be found in the story of Annette, and still eludes us.

CHAPTER VII

Jeffrey

TEN years before Wordsworth died an American reviewer wrote:

> It is not forgotten that Wordsworth's successive publications were assaulted by a flippant, heartless, and, in its recklessness of truth, a licentious criticism. . . . These criticisms may be preserved as curiosities of literature, and Lord Jeffrey has doubtless begun to have some misgivings about "the case" which his fierce surgery professed to abandon as "hopeless and incurable." Nay, the time may come when *his* memory may be chiefly perpetuated in the sinister fame which *The Excursion* will confer on that memorable phrase of his: "*This will never do.*" [1]

It would be hard to find a random bit of prophecy which has proved more accurate. Francis Jeffrey was one of the most brilliant figures of his time; a member of Parliament for the Perth burghs and later for Edinburgh, twice rector of the University of Glasgow, elevated to the Scotch bench and finally to the peerage. He died fully honored in 1850, the year of Wordsworth's death also. Yet the reviewer was right; those four ill-starred words are all that most men know of Francis Jeffrey. His injudicious sentence lives on to be read back to him at the Last Great Assize! For, as Quillinan wrote to Crabb Robinson long after 1814, "*It will do,* in spite of my Lord Jeffrey."

No one will ever know how deeply Wordsworth was hurt by Jeffrey's criticism, or how far his practice of poetry was modified in consequence of it. The journals and letters abound with wearisome statements that no quarterlies or

1. *The New York Review*, IV (1839), 20–21.

monthlies were let into the house. Yet the women of the family seem to have connived at a smuggler's trade in magazines, and to have read them with apprehensive curiosity. Wordsworth protested that he was immune to current notices of his work, but he protests too much, and many of the arrows seem to have got between the joints of his armor.[1] He always knew, in substance, what the reviewers were saying.

All other considerations to one side, hostile criticism was expensive; it cut down sales of the earlier volumes to a minimum. Wordsworth wrote to Francis Wrangham (November 4, 1807), "As Southey neatly says, 'They cannot blast our laurels, but they may mildew our corn.'" The journals and letters of the family are constantly harping on the need for money, on the hope vested in a new edition or a fresh work, and on expectations blighted by a volley of scorn. In his maturity the poet insisted — and Dorothy repeatedly confirms the statement — that he had no wish to print and did so only because he needed the royalties. For a quarter of a century Wordsworth had a money grievance against Jeffrey and did not hesitate to voice it. Jeffrey refused to be impressed and celebrated the poverty of great poets, a poverty which he was quite willing that they should freely enjoy in his stead. If Wordsworth was mercenary, Jeffrey was callous, and neither of the protagonists comes off well in their acrimonious discussion of an author's earnings. Wordsworth eventually made money, as the times went a good deal of money, out of his poems, but not until Jeffrey had left *The Edinburgh* and gone back to the law.[2]

1. *Blackwood's Edinburgh Magazine*, II (1817), 204. "The wit of the Edinburgh Reviewer has, I imagine, left such a scar on the liver of the Laker, that the discharge of bile and *sanies* is not chronic but continuous."
2. Wordsworth wrote to Francis Wrangham circa 1811 that up to that date the entire proceeds from his work had been less than £140. In 1838 he said, in a letter to Gladstone, that within the previous three years his writings had yielded him £1500.

There are some creations in this world of which we can only say that they are "out of nothing." Francis Jeffrey created the modern magazine and its editorial office out of nothing. *The Edinburgh Review* was without literary forbears; there was nothing in the way of existing publications to suggest or to require it. It was an original creation, conceived in the brains of a few idle young blades who were out for a literary lark.

When we compare their energetic journal with any one of the earlier periodicals we see how radical it was. Take, for example, any number of *The Monthly Magazine* — perhaps the most considerable of *The Edinburgh*'s predecessors — for the year 1800. What are its contents? Long letters from correspondents, the sort of thing that today is sent to *The Times* — travel papers of meager interest — anecdotes of prominent personages — lists of diseases in London, "Haemopte, 2; Prurigo, 3" — theater notices — new patents — casualties in London — lists of bankruptcies and dividends — marriages and deaths in London — provincial occurrences, with marriages and deaths in the counties — occasional articles on "The Flight of Birds," "The Climate of North America," "The State of Public Affairs." Of serious criticism of current English literature there was none.

Such was the state of journalism when Sydney Smith proposed to a half dozen friends met in his flat of an evening that they should start a review of their own. They were all young men; Allen, the oldest, was thirty-two, Smith thirty-one, Jeffrey twenty-nine, and the others in the early twenties. It all reads — in Cockburn's *Life of Lord Jeffrey* — very much like an undergraduate rag. There is the same suggestion of irresponsibility, a desire to shock and tease, and a determination to run no personal risks in so doing. The question of money did not interest them, provided they could pay expenses; it was to be "all gentlemen and no pay." The editors, who were to be also the contributors, were to conceal their identity, and contributions were to be unsigned. Once the *Review* was actually going, the meetings of the group had the quality of a conspiracy against the public weal; the perpetrators came singly by dark alleys and back doors to the printing-office where they read proofs of their articles and assembled the whole.

Jeffrey was skeptical. He gave their venture four numbers at the most. His pessimism was entirely in character, as he always lived "in a state of lively argumentative despair." No one was more surprised than he when *The Edinburgh Review* suddenly became a success. Its creators had not mistaken the time, but they had underrated their public. "There were reviews in England," says Lord Cockburn, "but, though respectable according to the notions of that time of critical respectability, they merely languished in decent feebleness. . . . It was an entire and instant change of everything the public had been accustomed to in that sort of composition. The old periodical opiates were extinguished at once." Jeffrey, who had entered into the venture for fun while waiting for a law practice, soon found himself editor-in-chief. The original group broke up after a year or so, and he was left in sole charge, giving to *The Edinburgh* the mark of his versatility and high spirits.

So far as Wordsworth is concerned, *The Edinburgh Review* of those years is remembered for its merciless criticism of the poet. Jeffrey had run foul of his victim in a review of Southey's *Thalaba*, which appeared in the first number. He returned more than once to the direct attack in the next twenty years, and even when he was discussing other authors it was hard for him to keep his itching hands off Wordsworth, since he had elected to make Wordsworth a test case for his criticism of current poetry.

In justice to Jeffrey it should be said that *The Edinburgh Review*, under his editorship, was a thoroughly progressive

journal. The urbane contempt which he felt for the Westmorland yokel who persisted in writing rustic verses is not
the dominant tone of the *Review*. In general the *Review*
espoused liberal causes, and was often found fighting on
the unpopular side. Jeffrey knew what it was to defend an
under-dog. He pamphleteered over twenty-five years for
the abolition of the slave trade, and moved sympatheti-
cally with the changes which led to the electoral reforms of
the 1830's.

As for the French wars, Jeffrey's hatred of France and
Napoleon was as cordial as Wordsworth's. But unlike
Wordsworth he stoutly combated that "craven fear of our
own countrymen which was the unhappy legacy of the
French Revolution." In this matter he comes off as much
more of a man than the poet. His words to Horner, in
1815, show him to have been the type of intellectual whom
the World War discovered among us a century later: "I
hate Bonaparte, because he makes me more afraid than
anybody else; and seems more immediately the cause of my
paying income-tax, and having my friends killed by dysen-
teries and gun-shot wounds, and making my country unpopular, grabbing, and servile, and everything I do not
wish it to be." The premises of the *Review*'s condemnation
of Wordsworth were not, therefore, a difference of basic
convictions about the values of life. Both men were supposedly protagonists for the people; each loathed France;
and at the time Jeffrey began to take exception to Wordsworth's verse the latter had not become a pronounced
Tory. Jeffrey's distaste for his victim was honestly academic; it was not politics in disguise.

His criticism of Wordsworth deserves a thorough re-
appraisal. The flippant first sentence of the review of *The
Excursion* is by no means the whole story. The difficulty
is that Jeffrey's treatment of Wordsworth cannot be isolated from his other editorial concerns or from the larger
strategy which began to take form once *The Edinburgh*

begot imitators and rivals. When modern students refer to the criticism of Wordsworth by his contemporaries, they cite their sources as if they existed *in vacuo* and pay no attention to the editorial policies which had determined in advance their general tenor. There was, in truth, a pretty war afoot, and Wordsworth was in the unfortunate position of a civilian strayed into no-man's land between the lines. The snipers on one side regarded him as a suspicious character; potential friends on the other side dared not come to his rescue for fear of exposing themselves to the galling fire of their adversaries. You do not get the connotation of any single journalistic criticism of Wordsworth from 1802 until about 1830 unless you know its source and read between the lines the editorial policy being pursued.

The Edinburgh Review had been founded in 1802. Late in life Jeffrey said that he once told Sir Walter, "The Review has but two legs to stand on, Literature is no doubt one of them: but its *Right leg* is politics." This right leg was not political-in-general, it was stoutly Whig. Plainly a Tory counterblast was needed, and it appeared in the form of *The Quarterly Review*, launched in 1809. The retort was from the outset reputable and had to be reckoned with thereafter. Lord Cockburn says that *The Quarterly* was Jeffrey's "first, and indeed throughout the whole of his editor-ship, his only formidable rival." Jeffrey, who loved a good fight, welcomed his opponent. He writes to Horner:

I have seen the Quarterly this morning. It is an inspired work, compared with the poor prattle of Cumberland. But I do not think it very formidable; and were it not for our offences, I should have no fear about its consequences. . . . My natural indolence would have been better pleased not to be always in sight of an alert and keen antagonist. But I do rejoice at the prospect of this kind of literature, and shall be proud to have set an example.

Blackwood's Edinburgh Magazine followed in 1817. It also was extreme Tory, but aimed to be more like a flying squadron and less like a heavy battalion than *The Quarterly Review*. It was to be a monthly, capable of swifter movement than the two heavier quarterlies. It hoped by sudden flank movements to be able to dislodge *The Edinburgh*, a feat which *The Quarterly* had been unable to achieve by frontal attack. Moreover *The Quarterly* had been grave in style and had tried to counter Jeffrey's wit with a deliberate solemnity. The attempt had not succeeded. *Blackwood's*, by its own confession, proposed to be "not so ponderous, more nimble, more frequent, more familiar" than its Tory senior, — in short more like Jeffrey. Furthermore, the prefatory advertisement in the first number announced frequent "notices of articles contained in the most celebrated periodical publications." In other words, when copy ran short, *Blackwood's* was prepared to play the vulture off such carrion as was the by-product of the rivalry of its two predecessors.

These three magazines occupied the center of the critical stage. There were other periodicals with quite distinct commitments, often ecclesiastical rather than political. *The Eclectic Review*, which gave Wordsworth much space, was mildly evangelical, and any surplus it earned was to go to the British and Foreign Bible Society. Wordsworth was dealt with accordingly. *The Monthly Review*, which had been running since 1749, was Whig and nonconformist. *The British Critic*, founded in 1793, was high church. In each instance the tenor of the literary criticisms was determined by some cause or party behind the journal. The periodicals of the first half of the last century were, in their editorial policies, much closer to the modern newspaper than to the modern magazine. The lesser journals took their cue from the three strong protagonists, seconding rather ineffectually the attack and counter-attack of the chief contestants.

It was Wordsworth's misfortune, given this battle array, that during all his early years nothing like a dispassionate criticism of his work was possible. The vigilant Jeffrey had happened to spy him roaming at large and had written him down as a fair target for his sharpshooting. One could hardly expect Jeffrey to understand Wordsworth or to like him, but he had no special animus against him. The vagrant Wordsworth had merely happened to catch his eye and to draw his fire. Having scored an initial hit, Jeffrey was committed to following up the attack as occasion offered. His writing, when addressed to Wordsworth, was adroit and captivating. His manner set the pattern for all adverse criticism of the poet, and his imitators were many. The journals of the period abound with the attempts of less clever men to copy his style. These efforts are both ludicrous and pathetic. In particular, "Pierce Pungent," who wrote for *Fraser's Magazine*, affected a super-Jeffrey style. This, for example, is his concluding criticism of the *Lucy* poems:

Don't you see that the rolling lady being dead cannot "feel," as Mr. Wordsworth profoundly says — that she unfortunately has not the least "motion" now, nor "no force," because, as we said, she is a dead woman, and "neither hears nor sees" — a "thought" by the bye which could never have occurred to any one speaking of the defunct, but the original mind of Mr. Wordsworth. As for the next stanza, wherein the defunct lady is so poetically represented to be, till this day, rolling round and round with the twirling globe, once every twenty four hours, along with rocks, and stones, and other hard substances; the thought has, we lament, made no particular impression upon us. . . . But let the lady roll away, rocks, and stones, and trees, and all!

When we find in the family journals and letters notices of Wordsworth's despair of contemporary criticism we should realize that this passage is typical of the treatment to which he was constantly subjected. Such, however, was the great Jeffrey's reputation that his understudies found a ready market for their wares, and the little Jeffreys were able to make a Roman holiday of Wordsworth at any time during the first quarter of the century.

One might expect that the Tory *Quarterly* would have come to Wordsworth's defense. It made desultory and half-hearted attempts to do so.[1] But Jeffrey had made Wordsworth such a figure of fun that it was hard to persuade the general reader to take him seriously. *Blackwood's*, being Tory, Anglican, anti-Jeffrey, and therefore theoretically pro-Wordsworth, tended to over-bid its hand. Thus in the notice of *Peter Bell* the reviewer apostrophizes the tinker's ass as "the fine and picturesque animal that occupies an important place in the story." The attempt to out-Wordsworth Wordsworth was no more successful than the endeavor to out-Jeffrey Jeffrey. Praise became so fulsome that it ceased to be criticism and crystallized into a kind of cult-language. The chant of the Wordsworthians was even worse than Jeffrey's profanity:

Here [in the *Ecclesiastical Sonnets*] we see the highest intellect bowing down in reverence and adoration before the spirit of Christianity — the most splendid imagination overpowered by its sanctities. . . . Here we see that genius can conceive no image so august, no emotion so affecting, as those that rise up at the feet of the altar. (*Blackwood's*, August, 1822)

The Eclectic Review, taking its cue from evangelical piety, found Wordsworth sadly wanting in a knowledge of the plan of salvation. It quotes Christopher North as doubting whether there was a Bible in poor Margaret's cottage, — "We doubt so too, and have not found much of the 'true cross' among all his trees."

1. So Dorothy writes (February, 1815) of an "encomiastic" notice of *The Excursion* in *The Eclectic Review* that "it will do less harm than the feeble praise of the *Quarterly*."

Is it [*The Excursion*] *true?* Is it *all?* True it undoubtedly is to a certain extent; but as undoubtedly it is not all. . . . We do not mean to infer that Mr. Wordsworth excludes from his system the salvation of man, as revealed in the Scriptures, but it is evident that he has not made "Jesus Christ the chief corner stone" of it; otherwise, throughout this admirable poem, he would not so seldom, or rather so slightly have alluded to "redemption in his blood." (*The Eclectic Review*, January, 1815)

From such comments we learn nothing about the poetical merits of the *Ecclesiastical Sonnets* or of *The Excursion*; we merely learn that *Blackwood's Magazine* was Tory and high church, and that *The Eclectic Review* was low church and evangelical. It is not enough, in studying the criticism of Wordsworth by his contemporaries, to cite a review; its source and setting must be identified and the resultant inferences drawn from its origin in either the Whig or the Tory camp, in the high church or the low church. In the main, over the first third of the century, the question comes down to this: Is the reviewer the formidable Jeffrey himself? is he imitating Jeffrey? or is he opposing Jeffrey?

The first dispassionate criticism of Wordsworth in the journals of the time was a series of four articles by John Wilson, which appeared in *Blackwood's* for September–December, 1829. These papers, because they were detached and written neither in blame nor in praise, mark the turn of the tide in Wordsworth's favor and from that time on it flooded strong. Thereafter Wordsworth gained followers by the hundreds, and, what was important from his own viewpoint, he began to see substantial sales. The early 1830's produced an increasing number of intelligent and discriminating reviews of the poet's work, which may be found variously in all the magazines of the period. The old editorial antipathies were spent or had lost their meaning. Even *The Edinburgh* of the poet's later years was quite as apt to approve as to condemn. Wilson's four

papers marked the beginning of this happier era. Why has
no one pointed out the significance of their date? They
began to appear in September, 1829. Jeffrey resigned the
editorship of *The Edinburgh Review* in June, 1829. Plainly
the two events fall within a *post hoc propter hoc* sequence
of cause and effect. So long as Jeffrey was in the office of
The Edinburgh he had, by right of initial conquest and
eminent domain, more or less arbitrary control of Wordsworth's literary fortunes. He invited imitators, and dis-
couraged opponents. Wordsworth's rise to fame dates
from the day Jeffrey gave up journalism for law.[1] We can
only say that the critic had kept the creator waiting for
recognition an unduly long time.

Francis Jeffrey, as we meet him in his contributions to
The Edinburgh, was a gay and versatile man, utterly without malice. His criticisms were pointed, but never poi-
soned at their tip. We do him a grave injustice if we think
of him as a medieval inquisitor torturing inoffensive poets.
His reviews were uniformly suggestive and often penetrating. Lord Cockburn in the *Life* attempts to clear
Jeffrey of the charges of malignity so often brought against
him. He says that by the very act of publishing an author
files a petition for notice. The critic, thus subpoenaed,
"assumes the censor's chair, and, concealed, has to examine and announce the character of every book that
stands before him for its doom." The reviewer comes after
the author and is apt to be the abler of the two. Nevertheless, the critic is only human and like all censors prefers
the discovery of faults to that of excellence. Once started
on his course, he makes the most of human frailty, not for
the delight of tormenting, but for the luxury of exercising
his skill in his chosen field. Jeffrey was not immune to the
temptation, yet, when he gave way to it,

1. Miss Edith Batho in *The Later Wordsworth* thinks that the tide had turned
ten years earlier. I doubt it. Wordsworth had devotees by 1820, but few dispassionate critics.

it was generally from mere lightness of spirit. Totally devoid of ill nature, and utterly unconscious of any desire to hurt, he handled the book as a thing to be played with; without duly considering that the gay and moral pleasantry of Horace might produce as much distress as the declamatory weight of Juvenal.

Such is Lord Cockburn's brief for Francis Jeffrey. Both were lawyers and judges and saw their world as magistrates on duty. There is in the biographer, as there was in his subject, a hint of the policeman whose business it is to ask vagrant characters to identify themselves.

As for Jeffrey's reviews of Wordsworth, they were by no means his sole stock-in-trade. While he was editor of the *Review*, he contributed two hundred articles on a hundred different subjects. Their titles indicate the range of his interests: "Voyages to North America," "Paley's Theology," "Travels in Egypt," "Abolition of the Slave Trade," "Cochin China," "Court Reforms," "Quakerism," "Household Furniture," "Health and Longevity," "Vaccination," "Ancient Armor," "Prison Discipline," "Phrenology," "Naval Tactics." Nor did Jeffrey confine himself to Wordsworth when he turned to current poetry. There are in *The Edinburgh Review* from 1802 through 1829 only four articles directly addressed to Wordsworth's work, as against eight reviews of Byron. One gets the impression that after 1815 Jeffrey deliberately avoided Wordsworth, either because he was afraid of saying too much or because he feared that he might have made a literary blunder in the position he had already taken. In a review of Byron's *Cain* written in 1822 he says:

There is nothing so certain, we take it, as that those who are the most alert in discovering the faults of a work of genius, are the least touched with its beauties; and seem more envious to be *safe*, than original. . . . Thus, the dread of ridicule, which they have ever before their eyes, represses all the emotions, on the expression of which their success entirely depends. . . . There is great want of magnanimity, we think, as well as of wisdom, in this sensitiveness to blame; and we are convinced that no modern author will ever write with the grace and vigour of the older ones, who does not write with some portion of their fearlessness, and indifference to censure. Courage, in short, is at least as necessary as genius to the success of a work of the imagination.

I find it hard to put away a suspicion that Jeffrey wrote the lines to himself and to Wordsworth, hoping that the intimate reference might be discovered beneath the impersonal law. He seems here to be visiting the enemy by night to give him aid and comfort. He is bidding Wordsworth have courage to play the man because he fears lest his own "vivacities" may have impaired the poet's self-assurance and have contributed to the decline which he was generous enough to regret.

We do Jeffrey a further injustice if we assume that he singled Wordsworth out as the sole butt for his critical high spirits. His gleeful detraction was meted out impartially to many victims. We remember some of the savage things he said about Wordsworth; we have forgotten, or we never knew, what he said of other poets of the time. Nothing that he wrote about Wordsworth is as cruel as his description of Coleridge, "going up in an air-balloon filled with the fetid gas from writings of Jacob Behmen, and coming down in a parachute made of the soiled leaves of the Morning Post." Not only so, but he could be as wrong about other poems as about *The Excursion*. So, of *Christabel*, its "*profound Bathos* is wholly bottomless"; and of *Kubla Khan*, written after a drug taken for sleeplessness, "the lines here given smell strongly of the anodyne." The volume which first contained these poems was dismissed as "one of the most notable pieces of impertinence of which the press has lately been guilty." Jeffrey was even harder on Byron, for here his raillery sobered into moral indignation. Byron's tragedies are "a tissue of wearisome and unimpassioned declamations," his style is "heavy, verbose, and inelegant," his plots are "lengthened out by large preparations for catastrophes that never arrive," over all there is "a varnish of voluptuousness on the surface and a canker of misanthropy at the core"; and "the world will weary at last of the most energetic pictures of outlaws and their mistresses." Wordsworth may have been handled roughly, but he was in good company and fared no worse than his peers.

On the credit side of his account with Wordsworth, Jeffrey conscientiously posted many items in the poet's favor. He had occasion, when his review of *The Excursion* was reprinted in the collected *Contributions to the Edinburgh Review* (1844), to reconsider his treatment of Wordsworth. In a prefatory note to the reprinted article he generously makes amend for the "vivacities of expression" and the "asperity" which had led him to speak "rather too bitterly and confidently" of Wordsworth's faults. At the same time he stands manfully by the critical position taken thirty years earlier, insisting that he had loved many of the attributes of Wordsworth's genius and had not been penurious or grudging in allowing the beauty of much of his work.

The pages of *The Edinburgh* bear Jeffrey out in his contention. He grants to Wordsworth "gleams of fancy or feeling"; he listens with "far deeper delight to the songs of his mountain solitude"; he looks with pleasure on "his mellow pictures of simple happiness and his lofty sketches of human worth and energy"; he finds in the *Lyrical Ballads* "a strong spirit of originality, of pathos, and natural feeling, recommended to all good minds by the clear impression of the amiable dispositions and virtuous principles of the author"; he credits *The Excursion* with "a very great number of single lines and images, that sparkle like gems in the desert"; in short, "the truth is that Mr. Wordsworth, with all his perversities, is a person of great powers." These are the high lights in the picture, and in justice to Jeffrey should not be overlooked.

On the other hand, the shadows were put in with a bold brush. His phrase about "the natural drawl of the lakers" is neatly turned and not impertinent. He hits off the situation slyly when he says of the divine intoxication of the poets that Wordsworth seems to have "dashed his Hippocrene with too large an infusion of lake water." And his description of the sixth book of *The Excursion* as "a choice obituary" is much too accurate. The more the pity that at times Jeffrey hit below the belt. The passages in his criticism of Wordsworth seriously open to question as breaches of good taste are those in which he twits the poet on his stamp-distributor's office. "The contact of the Stamp-office appears to have had a bad effect on Mr. Wordsworth . . . since he has openly taken to the office of a publican and exchanged the company of leech-gatherers for that of tax-gatherers." So of the tour of the Continent, Jeffrey suggests that Wordsworth should not have ignored Waterloo, since "his situation in the Stamp-office requires a few lines," but supposes that the poet is "blinded by the possession of a sinecure place in the Revenue department." All this was doubly uncalled for since Francis Jeffrey was more responsible than any other one man for Wordsworth's prolonged and thankless labors as a stamp clerk. Jeffrey should have been above personalities.

The points in common and the points at issue between the poet and the critic are reasonably clear. Jeffrey shared with Wordsworth a faith in Alison's *Essay on Taste*, and reviewed the essay favorably in *The Edinburgh*. In theory both men were agreed about the source of the pleasure which poetry gives; it has its origins in perceptions of beauty which may be reduced, by retracing our association of ideas, to simple past sensations.

We might suppose that Jeffrey would have run foul of Wordsworth over disputed theories of poetic diction. It is true that he did not like Wordsworth's choice of words, but he did not labor his dislike. He saw that Wordsworth's

diction was determined by its subjects, and he chose to
fight on the latter ground. In this he was right.

As for poetry in general, Francis Jeffrey had got off on
the wrong foot in his review of *Thalaba*:

> Poetry has this much, at least, in common with religion, that its
> standards were fixed long ago, by certain inspired writers, whose
> authority it is no longer possible to call into question, and that
> many profess to be entirely devoted to it, who have no *good
> works* to produce in support of their contentions. The catholic
> poetical church, too, has worked but few miracles since the first
> ages of its establishment.[1]

His only serious discussion of the vexed matter of poetic
diction is to be found where we should look for it, in his
review of the *Biographia Literaria*. He delivers himself
unequivocally on the issue which Coleridge had seen fit to
reopen:

> There is, no doubt, a simple and familiar language, common to
> almost all ranks, and intelligible through many ages, which is
> the best fitted for the direct expression of strong sense and deep
> passion, and which consequently is the language of the best
> poetry as well as of the best prose. But it is not the exclusive
> language of poetry. There is another language, peculiar to this
> manner of writing, which has been called *poetic diction* — those
> flowers of speech, which whether natural or artificial, fresh or
> faded, are strewed over the plainer ground which poetry has in
> common with prose; a paste of rich and honeyed words, like the
> candied coat of the auricula; a glittering tissue of quaint conceits
> and sparkling metaphors, crusting over the rough stalk of
> homely thoughts. . . . The beauty of poetic diction is, in short,
> borrowed and artificial.[2]

Jeffrey was writing in the aftermath of the eighteenth
century and his faith in the artifices of a passing day prevented him from seeing another dawn. Had he read Jef-

1. *The Edinburgh Review*, I (1802), 63.
2. *Ibid.*, XXVIII (1817), 512.

frey's criticism of the *Biographia Literaria*, Wordsworth
might have resurrected and invoked Beaupuy's words
about the peasant girl, "'Tis against *that* which we are
fighting." Jeffrey threw little light on the problem of the
right words for poetry and contented himself with genteel
reminiscences of a day that was already doomed. He did
not realize how low its sun was and how late its afternoon.

There are, however, two indictments of Wordsworth in
Jeffrey's criticism which were serious at the time, and
which, after the lapse of years, still keep their pertinence.

Jeffrey objected primarily to Wordsworth's choice of
mean and trivial subjects. He constantly returns to the
attack, even when Wordsworth is not his immediate victim. Thus he prefers Mr. Wilson's poems precisely because
Wilson "does not break out into ecstasies about spades or
sparrow's eggs — or men gathering leeches — or women in
duffle coats — or plates or porringers — or washing tubs
— or any of those baser themes which poetry was always
permitted to disdain without any impeachment of her affa-
bility, till Mr. Wordsworth thought fit to force her into an
acquaintance with them." The elaborations of the indictment are many and are done in Jeffrey's most vigorous
style. He rested his case against Wordsworth's practice in
matters of poetic diction on the subjects rather than on
the verbal style. He disliked the category of the homely,
the simple, and the rustic, from Wilkinson's spade through
The Excursion's pedlar.

There was, of course, a difference in the whole history
and the temperament of the two men. The life Jeffrey lived
and understood was that which he so earnestly recommended to Wordsworth for his salvation as a poet, —
"the ordinary, practical, and amiable life of social, intelligent, and affectionate men in the upper ranks of society."
Since these were the persons who read poetry, they were
also the persons to be included in poetry. Jeffrey was not
under the delusion that a poem must deal with "warlike

paladins, desperate lovers, and sublime ruffians." He did
not ask poetry to tell stories of "palaces, castles, camps,
tyrants, warriors, and bandits." If he loved Wordsworth
less, it was not that he loved Byron more. He quite understood that good poetry can be written about plain people.
In treating of Crabbe he always went out of his way to
commend him for succeeding where Wordsworth failed.
"Mr. Crabbe exhibits the common people of England
pretty much as they are." And these common people "as
they are" form a fit theme for poetry.

The delineation of all that concerns the lower and most nu-
merous classes of society, is, in this respect, on a footing with the
pictures of our primary affections — that their originals are
necessarily familiar to all men. . . . Every one understands
about cottages, streets, and villages: and conceives pretty cor-
rectly the character and condition of sailors, ploughmen, and
artificers. . . . The poets of the Village and the Borough will be
oftener and longer read than the poets of the Court and the
Camp.[1]

Why, then, did Jeffrey object to Wordsworth's poems on
such subjects? He is quite explicit on the matter. The
admixture of William Wordsworth in the finished poem is
disproportionately large; his

low bred heroes, and interesting rustics, have no sort of affinity
to the real vulgar of this world; they are imaginary beings, whose
characters and language are in contrast with their situation.[2]

The pedlar of *The Excursion* becomes the test case:

Why should Mr. Wordsworth have made his hero a super-
annuated Pedlar? What but the most wretched affectation, or
provoking perversity of taste, could induce any one to place his
chosen advocate of wisdom and virtue in so absurd and fan-
tastic a condition? Did Mr. Wordsworth really imagine, that
his favourite doctrines were likely to gain anything in point of

---

1. *The Edinburgh Review*, XVI (1810), 33–34.
2. *Ibid.*, I (1802), 67.

effort or authority by being put into the mouth of a person accustomed to higgle about tape, or brass sleeve buttons? . . . Is there anything in his learned, abstract, and logical harangues that savours of the calling that is ascribed to him? Are any of their materials such as a pedlar could possibly have dealt in? . . . A man who went about selling flannel and pocket-handkerchiefs in this lofty diction, would soon frighten away all his customers; and would pass infallibly either for a madman, or for some learned and affected gentleman, who, in a frolic, had taken up a character which he was peculiarly disqualified for supporting. The absurdity in this case, we think, is palpable and glaring; but it is exactly of the same nature with that which infects the whole substance of the work.[1]

Jeffrey does Wordsworth the justice of conceding that the poet was sincere in his association of deep emotions and universal truths with trivial occasions. He does not question Wordsworth's report of his thoughts and feelings in the presence of spades and tubs and sparrows' eggs. He merely insists that Wordsworth shall not expect or require others to feel the same way or to think his thoughts after him. No one can deny that Jeffrey has a case. We concede Michael, and Margaret, and the Cumberland Beggar, and the Highland Girl. In them Wordsworth succeeds. But we are also aware that Wordsworth is by no means successful in all his ventures, and that certain of them fail. There are border-line cases; the pedlar is one of them. Is Alice Fell a success, in that Wordsworth recreates for us her poignant cosmic tragedy? On the whole, yes; but there are moments when we wonder, with a critic of the time, whether the sorrow is so great that "her tears should be preserved in a bottle."

It should be said in Wordsworth's behalf that he was experimenting with new subjects for poetry, or at least according them a novel treatment in verse, and that uniform success was not to be expected. The striding edge

1. *The Edinburgh Review*, XXIV (1814), 29-30.

between the sublime and the ridiculous along which he
made his way was sharp, and the slightest slip was costly.
His own lack of humor was serious, and the ease with which
he has lent himself to parody is witness to the precarious-
ness of his position. We need Jeffrey to remind us that not
every humble or trivial subject which Wordsworth touched
was apotheosized by him. He fails to make a poetic case
for his

> Negro Ladies in white muslin gowns!

Whatever our debt to Wordsworth, we should still thank
Jeffrey for pointing out the frequent excess of imagination
in the treatment of an elected theme, an excess which
makes the result a failure because of a felt incongruity between the inciting subject and the finished poem.

Finally, Jeffrey objected to the predominance of "the
system" in Wordsworth's work. He did not find the poems
spontaneous or inevitable; he was keenly aware of their
experimental nature. He announced his dissent in his review of Southey's *Thalaba*, and elaborated it in the subsequent papers on Wordsworth. He distrusted system-
mongering in verse, and, when he read his Wordsworth,
the system was so much to the front that he could not see
the poetry. Jeffrey thus identified the one important issue,
and we must admire the acumen which prompted him to
fight on what is still the most disputed ground in the criticism of Wordsworth. He is in this matter the precursor of
Matthew Arnold and an opponent of that Wordsworthianism which Leslie Stephen was to defend.

How far may Jeffrey and his disciples have changed
Wordsworth's practice in the writing of poetry? It is impossible to say. Wordsworth's later regrets that he had
ever written the prefaces and essays-supplementary indicate that criticism did not leave him untouched. Yet having written them, he persisted in reprinting them in every
collected edition of his poems, and there they still are. He

ceased, however, after about 1814 to give the reader prose
first-aid and left the poems to explain themselves, — a
wise decision. It is more than probable that Jeffrey contributed to that decision. Furthermore, the subjects of the
later poems during the years of the anti-climax do not run
true to earlier form. One has only to glance over the titles
to see the difference. *To the Lady Mary Lowther*, *To the
Lady E. B. and the Hon. Miss P.*, *On the Death of His
Majesty* (*George* III), — these would not have appeared
in the *Lyrical Ballads*. Whether Jeffrey is chargeable for
them or whether they made him any happier, we cannot
know.

As for Jeffrey, his pharmacopoeia was exhausted by
1814:

> The case of Mr. Wordsworth, we perceive, is now manifestly
> hopeless; and we give him up as altogether incurable, and be-
> yond the power of criticism. We cannot indeed altogether admit
> taking precautions now and then against the spread of the
> malady; — but for himself, though we shall watch the progress
> of his symptoms as a matter of professional curiosity and in-
> struction, we really think it is right not to harness him any
> longer with nauseous remedies, — but rather to throw in cordials
> and lenitives, and wait in patience the natural termination of
> the disorder.[1]

If it was impossible for Jeffrey to be patient with Wordsworth, it is hard for us not to be impatient with Jeffrey,
when he says of the ode on the *Intimations of Immortality*
that it is "illegible and unintelligible" and that he can
"pretend to give no analysis or explanation of it." It may
well be that there were certain subjects to which Francis
Jeffrey was born blind. If not we can only say that confronted with much that is best in Wordsworth he deliberately put out his own eyes. The critical light that should
have been in him was too often darkness. He lives today

1. *The Edinburgh Review*, XXIV (1814), 2.

by the reflected light which falls on him mainly from the
work of one whom he was too much a son of the decorous
eighteenth century to understand. Yet, I confess to a liking for Jeffrey the man, which I cannot pretend for Wordsworth. I should much rather have spent an evening with
him in Edinburgh, hearing the rapier play of his gay words,
than have sat at Town-end in "long barren silence,"
listening

> to the flapping of the flame,
> Or kettle whispering its faint undersong.

Even Crabb Robinson, who knew Wordsworth well, con-
tinually reverts to the rather rude notice which the poet
served on his acquaintances to stay away or to keep still.

CHAPTER VIII

The System

WE HAVE been reviewing at length the several causes to which Wordsworth's decline has been assigned. They have been, variously: his premature aging, his break with Coleridge, his change of political affiliation, his affair with Annette Vallon, and his intimidation by Francis Jeffrey. Any or all of them may have contributed to his impairment. Each was an intimate matter, penetrating deep into his life, and none of these experiences can be dissected out of his history leaving an unimpaired man. Yet there is reason to doubt whether we have yet found the true source of Wordsworth's anti-climax. Of the causes considered thus far, the unexciting matter of his late literary arrival and his premature old age seems the most pertinent. But even that fact does not finally dispose of our perplexity. Is there any other possible explanation of Wordsworth's decline?

I think there is, and that Francis Jeffrey fastened upon it in his review of *The Excursion*:

> The very quantity, too, that he has written, and is at this moment working up for publication upon the old pattern, makes it almost hopeless to look for any change of it. All this is so much capital already sunk in the concern; which must be sacrificed if it is to be abandoned.[1]

In any consideration of Jeffrey's criticism we should remember that his objection to Wordsworth was based on

1. *The Edinburgh Review*, XXIV (1814), 2.

his dislike and his distrust of the poet's choice of subjects for verse. He thought it a pity that so many talents should have been invested in a venture which had to operate with such meager material. That is what he means by capital sunk in the concern.

Meanwhile Jeffrey's metaphor is illuminating. We are willing to concede what Jeffrey never conceded, that the system had its merits. But even if it had merits, was it not bound to prove a liability in the end precisely because it was a system? In matters of this sort — poetry, religion, and the like — it is dangerous to elaborate a theory first and then to require the theory to beget experience. Abstract theories are once removed from the facts which they profess to explain and normally follow those facts in time. If they antedate the experiences which are their subject they eventually prove to be sterile. It seems clear, therefore, that in the conversations with Coleridge out of which the matured scheme for poetry came, Wordsworth was storing up trouble for the future. The theory, as he formulated it, seemed to throw much light on his own past thoughts and emotions, but his supply of past experiences was limited. After they had been used up the theory had to make its living off the land. It was, therefore, a risky venture which tied up Wordsworth's entire poetic capital with a single system of esthetics. The initial experiment proved successful and remains so to this day; but the capital eventually became unproductive because of a dearth of the necessary subject-matter.

In his review of Southey's *Thalaba* (October, 1802) Jeffrey had already identified Wordsworth and his neighbors as "a sect." Whenever he returned to the battle, he labored the point that their poems were "written avowedly for the purpose of exalting a system." Jeffrey's word "system" became a commonplace in the contemporary criticism and compelled the poet's apologists to explain and to defend a practice which his opponents condemned,

— the custom of writing verses to bear out a preconceived theory about the content of poetry and the manner of its composition. Neither friend nor foe could deny the fact, and each dealt with it in his own way, the friends less effectually than the foes. Therefore criticism addressed itself to this vulnerable spot in the poet's armor and that of his defenders. By Wordsworth's system Jeffrey and his fellow-critics understood a kind of poetry which chose as its subject incidents from "humble and rustic life" and which used "the language of conversation in the middle and lower classes of society." The innovation was so radical that the reviewers had no need to go further. Poetry on these terms was not possible. But Wordsworth's choice of subjects and of words was not the heart of his poetic doctrine, it was merely the corollary of a highly involved theory about the genesis of poetry and the nature of the poetic act. Current criticism, however, did not need to go back to the first article of Wordsworth's faith; popular taste being what it was, the corollary was enough to damn the venture.

We shall not understand Wordsworth's meager fortunes from 1798 until about 1830, unless we realize how large the controversy over the system bulked in notices of his work, and how generally it was condemned.

Jeffrey is explicit:

With Mr. Wordsworth and his friends, it is plain that their peculiarities of diction are things of choice, and not of accident. They write as they do upon principle and system; it evidently costs them pain to keep *down* to the standard which they have proposed for themselves.[1]

The Dublin University Magazine (June, 1835) tells us that

The preface to the Lyrical Ballads, rather than anything in the poems themselves, produced the contest which has been prolonged into our own times. . . . The *trifles* Mr. Wordsworth

---

1. *The Edinburgh Review*, XI (1807), 217.

published in his earlier volume would have been allowed to produce their natural effect of giving great pleasure, had it not been
for his own *trifling* about them. . . . We wish that all the prose
may be excluded from the future editions of his poems. The
purpose which it was intended to answer, was in its nature temporary and the very existence of the attacks upon Mr. Wordsworth would already have been forgotten, had it not been for
his own essays, defensive and aggressive.

The Edinburgh (January, 1833) reviewed the historic
encounter three or four years after Jeffrey gave up his
editorship:

A great part of the opposition which Mr. Wordsworth's poetry
has had to encounter, is the consequence of the extent to which
he has reduced his theory to practice [i.e. an identical language
of prose and poetry]. In our opinion the slowness with which his
works have made their way up to an influence and reputation
which their beauties were sure of ultimately commanding, is
most naturally accounted for by the weary length to which,
passage after passage, a doctrine of this sort systematically entertained must often throw its shade.

It was Hazlitt's opinion that Wordsworth

affects a system without an intelligible clue to one, and, instead
of unfolding a principle in various and striking lights, repeats
the same conclusions till they become flat and insipid.

John Wilson ("Christopher North"), who was friendly
and wished to be appreciative, felt that "the idea of fabri-
cating poetry according to a set theory is an unhappy one,"
and could not escape the conviction that "there is something rotten in the state of Wordsworth." [1] A reviewer of
The Prelude is irked by its content and argument: "From
the minstrel we want, not philosophy, but a story and a
tune." [2] The predominance of the system made Wordsworth, in Jeffrey's eyes, "a bad imitator of the worst of his

1. *Blackwood's Edinburgh Magazine*, XXVI (1829), 593.
2. *The Dublin University Magazine*, XXXVI (1850), 329.

former faults";[1] in the words of another critic it turned
him into a mountain climber out early and late doing practice climbs.[2] The last metaphor is uncomfortably accurate, and should be matched by James Russell Lowell's
comment, in his presidential address before the Wordsworth Society:

> Too often, when left to his own resources, and to the conscien-
> tious performance of the duty laid upon him to be a great poet
> *quand même*, he seems diligently intent on producing fire by the
> primitive method of rubbing the dry sticks of his blank verse
> one against the other, while we stand in shivering expectation
> of the fire that never comes.

The references indicate how much the system was to the
fore in the minds of the critics, and how difficult they found
it to condone. It delayed unduly long a true appreciation
of the poems. But that is for us an irrelevant matter, since
the poet eventually lived down his prefaces. The important question is this: Had the adoption of the system
unhappy consequences for Wordsworth himself? Was
there, to use Jeffrey's phrase, too much capital sunk in a
single venture? The answer, I think, is Yes. Within the
scope of the answer we shall probably find the true cause
of Wordsworth's dismal anti-climax.

Wordsworth's theory of the genesis and nature of poetry
was derived from the current psychology of his day. That
psychology, begun with Locke, had been developed by
David Hartley in the early half of the eighteenth century.
Hartley had been abridged, republished, and provided with
explanatory essays by Joseph Priestley in 1775. A second
edition of *Hartley's Theory of the Human Mind on the
Principles of the Association of Ideas* had been printed for
Priestley by Johnson in 1790. Johnson's shop in St. Paul's
Churchyard was one of the places where Wordsworth fore-

1. *The Edinburgh Review*, XI (1807), 231.
2. *The British and Foreign Review*, XIV (1843), 11.

gathered with his malcontent friends. If he did not meet Priestley there in person, he must have come across Priestley's edition of Hartley. If so, he went forearmed with Hartley to his first meeting with Coleridge.[1] And at some time before 1798 he seems to have read Alison's *Essay on Taste*, which was the standard manual of esthetics for such persons as followed the lead of Locke, Hartley, and Priestley.

The psychology which Wordsworth thus accepted denied the existence of innate ideas.[2] In unself-conscious infancy and in unreflective childhood — so runs the theory — the outer world makes strong impressions upon us through the senses. These sense impressions leave a deposit in the mind in the form of simple ideas, which are nothing but the memory of the prior simple sensations. Simple ideas, associated with one another in subsequent thinking, result in complex ideas, which are the normal content of our mature thought. To understand any one of our complex ideas, we must resolve it first into its component simple ideas and then refer the simple ideas to their origin in sensation.

The enjoyment which we get from a work of art, that is, "the pleasure of taste," is thus discovered to be grounded in sensation. To identify the sources of our pleasures of taste we must reverse the process of association, and dissociate our complex ideas into their sensational originals. Thus I see some brown autumnal landscape which gives me intense pleasure. If I try to identify the sources of my

1. In learning his Godwin, Wordsworth had learned, by inference, his Hartley as well. But I cannot resist the conclusion that Priestley's edition of Hartley must have been Wordsworth's source-book in psychology, since it bore Johnson's imprint. Coleridge was, according to Cottle, already a convert to Hartley. When Wordsworth and Coleridge met they must have had, therefore, a common familiarity with the theses which they eventually worked over for their own uses.

2. This whole matter is treated admirably and at length by Arthur Beatty, *William Wordsworth* (University of Wisconsin Studies, 1927), pp. 38–127. Professor Beatty's work is invaluable. But I have written my own account of Wordsworth's debt to Hartley and Alison after reading the original sources.

pleasure, I finally discover that the brownness, which particularly pleases me, is associated with the color of the skin of russet apples from a tree in my childhood home. My artistic satisfaction factors down, by the processes of analytic dissociation, to the nutty flavor of the brown apple, which I so enjoyed when I was a boy. Hartley, Alison, and their disciples, who referred esthetic pleasure to its origin in simple sensation, were always able to discover some such sensation as the first link in the chain which had ended in the pleasurable complex idea the artist had elaborated.

This theory of esthetics puts entirely out of bounds its classical opposite. According to the classical theory of esthetics, the pleasure which we derive from a work of art has no connection with our sensations and need not be referred back to them. It is an immediate reaction of the mind, which reads a plus sign before such facts, whether in nature or in the field of human invention, as give us congruous parts within an orderly whole. If I am a classicist, the pleasure which I get from the autumn landscape need not be referred to the flavor of russet apples, but comes from my perception of the fitness of the oak trees and their leaves, the dried ferns, and the yellowing grass, each to the other in a harmonious whole.

Now Wordsworth never consciously wrote poetry as a classicist, he always wrote as an associationist. True, many of his poems give an even greater pleasure to persons of the former persuasion than to those of the latter, but that is an accident and was no part of his intention. His prefaces and essays are tracts in defense of the esthetic theory which he had derived from Locke, Hartley, and Alison. So far as his own conscious method was concerned, he was self-exiled from the great classical tradition in art. This abnegation was to prove costly, since the English School of Taste became a dead-end in esthetics. It did not perpetuate itself at anything like the dimensions which it achieved in the late eighteenth century. Therefore, Wordsworth, like many another explorer on an unknown river, followed a fork which did not issue in the open ocean, but ended in a cul-de-sac of slack water.

Alison's *Essay on Taste* was written in 1790. With Priestley's edition of Hartley it was the source-book for the most important of all Wordsworth's prose apparatus, the preface to the second edition of the *Lyrical Ballads*. Anyone who will work through that *Essay* can see how closely, even slavishly, Wordsworth followed Alison's lead. Alison labors the importance of allowing complex ideas to associate themselves in the mind as they will. For this purpose a passive and vacant state of mind is the first essential. If we withdraw the mind from attention to external facts and leave it in a state of reverie, free to follow its own devices, it will go its way of unimpeded association until a certain mental excitement begins to communicate itself to our feelings. The idle and the unemployed are, therefore, the persons most likely to have the artist's experience of mental excitement and of heightened feelings. It is rather like mixing certain chemical elements; their combination gives you an attendant heat.

In the state of initial vacancy, of subsequent association of complex ideas, and of heightened feelings, imagination asserts itself, and artistic creation takes place. But the complex ideas employed for a work of art can always be reduced on examination to unmixed feelings of gayety, pathos, solemnity, and the like, which are derived from simple sensations. On this theory, it is not necessary that we should have our processes of association set in motion by the stimulus of some outer object, which is perceived to be like one that gave us a pleasurable sensation at a much earlier time in our lives. The mind, left to itself in reverie, will care for the matter adequately, and will work in faithful fidelity to the primal sensations which are the ground of all pleasure.

Alison elaborated Hartley in attaching to the senses of sight and hearing a preponderant importance for the artist. Hartley had said:

> The ideas of this sense [sight] are far more vivid and definite than those of any other; agreeably to which the word *idea* denoted these alone in its original and most peculiar sense. . . .
>
> Our stock of visible ideas may be considered as a key to a great part of our knowledge, and a principal source of invention in poetry, painting . . . and almost every other branch of the arts and sciences. . . .
>
> The corporeal pleasures from articulate sounds are either evanescent from the first, or however become so very early in life. By this means we are much better qualified to receive information, with mental pleasures and improvements from them; and the ear becomes like the eye, a method of perception suited to the wants of a spiritual being.
>
> The ideas of sight and hearing are the principal storehouse of the fancy or imagination; and the imaginative arts of painting and music stand in the same relation to them. Poetry comprehends both by talking in language, which is the general representative of all our ideas and affections.[1]

Two or three other theses of this psychology deserve mention. One concerns the excess of pleasure over pain in our human experience; pain is self-eliminating, a protective device which directs us automatically to objects which will yield us pleasure. Next, there is the stress upon the greater excellence of "moderate incitements" in fostering intellectual pleasures. And finally there is this ominous note, "The pleasures of imagination in general, as well as each particular set and individual, must decline at last from the nature of our frame." [2] Wordsworth accepted all these theories as proven dogmas and set to work with them.

---

1. Joseph Priestley, *Hartley's Theory of the Human Mind, On the Principle of the Association of Ideas; with Essays relating to the Subject of it*, second edition (London: J. Johnson, 1790). Hartley's work had been published in 1749, Priestley's first edition in 1775.   2. *Ibid.*, p. 256.

It would be redundant, even impertinent, to reprint at length the familiar passages in Wordsworth's prefaces which deal with the genesis of poetry. If the reader does not know them, he is referred to the originals. Assuming a familiarity with Wordsworth's theories, I propose certain comments upon them.

That Wordsworth had "read, marked, learned" his Hartley and Alison is beyond question. The similarity of their arguments and at certain points the identities of a technical vocabulary prove the point. For example, when he speaks of "fair trains of imagery" he had appropriated for his verse a phrase which Alison uses constantly. "In such trains of imagery, no labour or thought, or habits of attention are required; they rise spontaneously in the mind." This is Alison, but it might as well be Wordsworth. Indeed, one passes from Hartley and Alison to Wordsworth's explanatory prose without being aware of any transition. It is in all three instances an identical world. One writer speaks of "complex emotions," "the means by which taste may be corrected or improved," "trains of pleasing or solemn thought," "the vacant and unemployed," "the pleasures of imagination." A second speaks of "certain known habits of association," "the manner in which we associate our ideas in a state of excitement," "elementary feelings," "an overbalance of pleasure," "a lively sensibility." The third speaks of "simple ideas," "the associated circumstances of the pleasures," "our passions and affections," "sensible pleasures and pains," "the pleasures of imagination," "moderate incitements from the associated circumstances of former pleasurable states." [1] William, Dorothy, and Coleridge were once described as "three persons and one soul." With equal accuracy we might describe Hartley, Alison, and Wordsworth as three psychologists with a single system.

1. These are, in order, Alison, Wordsworth, Hartley.

Wordsworth's prose apparatus cannot be read, therefore, without constant resort to the glossary found in his sources. It may be said that he is using the vocabulary which all writers on esthetics must employ. But his words do not have today, unless checked by their sources, the connotation which he intended. Wordsworth says that a poet is a man who is "pleased with his own passions and volitions." What does he mean when he speaks of a "passion"? The answer is to be found in Priestley's introduction to Hartley, "When we say that any idea or circumstance excites a particular *passion*, it is explained by observing that certain feelings and emotions have formerly been connected with that particular idea or circumstance, which it has the power of recalling by association." What is a "volition"? "A *volition* is a modification of the passion of *desire*, exclusive of any tumultuous emotion which the idea of a favorite object not possessed may excite."

The identities of word and phrase are far too many to be accidental. Indeed, no one seriously supposes that they are mere coincidences. Hence Wordsworth's prefaces are not, as they stand, self-explanatory. To master his argument we need to know the technical meaning which he assigned to each of the terms he uses. How far he had "inwardly digested" his sources is a question. Wordsworth was never a systematic thinker of the first rank, and often made free use of abstractions which were clearer to their authors than to him. I have read the prefaces many times, and have to confess that I still find certain passages obscure. I sometimes suspect that the obscurity has its origins, not in my stupidity, but in Wordsworth's imperfect mastery of the theories which he proposed to vindicate. There is, in some passages, an opaqueness in his account of poetry which suggests that he was quoting words he had learned by rote but did not fully understand. If this be so, we should regard it as praise rather than blame, for it means that he was a poet before he was a psychologist.

Meanwhile Wordsworth took from his sources the axioms which were to determine the poetic experiment upon which he proposed to embark. There is, in the first place, the "wise passiveness" which he celebrates. The Quakers of his own day hailed that phrase as a vindication of their doctrines, and quietists ever since have found Wordsworth, at this point, peculiarly congenial. But *Expostulation and Reply* looks to Hartley, Priestley, and Alison for its ancestry rather than to George Fox. This wise passiveness was not so much a religious invitation to the Spirit of God as a psychological device for inducing poems. "It is upon the vacant and the unemployed," says Alison, "accordingly, that the objects of taste make the strongest impression." Hence "majestic indolence" becomes with Wordsworth, if not a virtue in itself, at least a necessary prelude to the pleasures of taste.

In the next place, Wordsworth's preference for sensations and simple ideas which come to us through the eye and the ear, rather than by taste, smell, and touch, is derived from Hartley. "She gave me eyes, she gave me ears," he says gratefully of Dorothy. That cannot have been the whole truth. His sister certainly directed his eyes to healing sights and his ears to soothing sounds, but his theoretical confidence in the primacy of the two senses came from the particular psychology he was employing. Hartley, and Wordsworth after him, may have been right in saying that our strongest impressions and our most important ideas come through seeing and hearing. But the point can be argued. We do not forget that for Marcel Proust the sense of taste was the medium by which he best recovered the distant past and gained such entrance as he achieved into the world of changeless reality. The famous incident of the madeleine dipped in tea falls well outside Hartley's doctrinaire psychology and Wordsworth's poetic usage.

Then there is Wordsworth's almost preposterous confidence in infancy. His speculative interest in children, and in particular in his own childhood, was far more a reasoned dogma than a spontaneous impulse. Here, in infancy and childhood, sense experiences are purest and ideas simplest. In mature persons complex ideas become, in their interrelations, so involved that it is difficult, indeed at times impossible, to reduce them to their primal terms and thus to recover by their free interplay emotions kindred to those which childhood knows. Hartley himself admitted the difficulty. Grown-up sophistication is a barren seed-ground for the arts. The simple sensations, and ideas of sensation which obtain in earliest life, either observed or remembered, are a much richer soil for the poet to till.

So, also, with Wordsworth's humble heroes and heroines of rustic life. It may be ungenerous to say that in daily life he took little or no interest in them, but plainly he looked on them as laboratory supplies rather than as friends. He tells us quite unequivocally that he chose this type because in such persons "the essential passions of the heart find a better soil" and "speak a plainer and more emphatic language"; because in them "the elementary feelings co-exist in a state of greater simplicity, and, consequently, may be more accurately contemplated, and more forcibly communicated." We are not in a position to deny his statement; presumably it is true. The steady drift of letters since Wordsworth's day has been in his direction. Nevertheless, his choice of human subjects was in the first instance a matter of finding material which should be suitable for his esthetic experiment. Wordsworth the poet employed the acquaintances of Wordsworth the neighbor for purposes which they could hardly have understood. To be blunt, he made copy of them.

Unlike many another writer who has used his neighbors as copy, Wordsworth does not leave them in a light less lovely than that which fell on them from common day. It was his conscious purpose to make us feel that "we are greater than we know," and this purpose he extended to his subjects as well as to his readers. The humble originals of Michael and Margaret were transfigured by his imagination, yet in their transfiguration still remain faithful to themselves. We mark no grave discrepancy, and in imputing to their lives meanings and values which his imagination discovered in them, Wordsworth does not make the truth of poetry a falsehood of fact. His neighbors, if they ever recognized themselves in the poems, must have been puzzled, but they can never have been angered. There was no caricature or satire; nor did the poet content himself with paying his heroes and heroines the measured due of a pitiless realism. He looked on their shield from the golden side, and gave substance to hidden virtues which his insight discerned. No human theme that Wordsworth touched was debased because his imagination had been fixed steadily upon it.

Nevertheless, when as a mature poet Wordsworth

> descried in distant sky,
> A solitary object and sublime,
> Above all height, —

a shepherd on the horizon of his world, — his relation to that figure was no longer direct, immediate, intuitive. It was reflective, self-conscious, and highly technical. To revive Aristotle's distinction between those things which are illiberal and those which are liberal, Wordsworth "used" rather than "enjoyed" the shepherd. There is, for all the poet's profession of sympathy with his neighbors, an illiberality in his treatment of them which he cannot wholly conceal. In *The Old Cumberland Beggar* this illiberality breaks through the technique of composition into the argument of the poem. The beggar is to be tolerated, even welcomed, because

> the villagers in him
> Behold a record which together binds
> Past deeds and offices of charity,
> Else unremembered, and so keeps alive
> The kindly mood.

Here the doctrinaire Wordsworth betrays and in a measure justifies his poetic practice of finding esthetic pleasure in the contemplation of humble figures. If the beggar kept the spring of charity open in the hearts of the villagers, he also stirred the waters in the well of verse by which William Wordsworth sat. He was doubly justified in the economy of things. It was a happy accident for Wordsworth that the neighbors whom he had known first and best proved at a much later time such proper grist for the mills of Hartley's psychology and Alison's esthetics.

Then there is the all-important matter of the lapse of time necessary to the making of a poem, between the moment when its subject is first given as a simple sensation and the hour when imagination recovers it and vests it with a kindred emotion. "Successful composition generally begins" only at this later time. The poet is a person who is affected by absent things as though they were present, and the gulf which absence creates is, with Wordsworth, a matter of time rather than of space. His best subjects he found in past time, and his most characteristic poetry might be described by the caption which Marcel Proust chose for his vast literary enterprise, *A la recherche du temps perdu*, "Remembrance of Things Past." Wordsworth was a poet

> not used to make
> A present joy the matter of my Song.

During the golden decade this practice was at first a conscious choice, but it tended to become a mental habit. He is explicit (in *The Waggoner*) when he tells us that his inspiration, and therefore his theme,

> will sometimes leap
> From hiding places ten years deep.

Poems are not spawned in an instant; they require long years of gestation. There is no hope of poetry while sensation is strong upon us; the motions of sense must be suspended, we must be "laid asleep in body." Perhaps the finest account of this distinction is that in the sixth book of *The Prelude*, which tells of the crossing of the Alps. The passage describes one of the first moments when Wordsworth realized that, before imagination can lift like "an unfathered vapour," the light of sense must have gone out. A time element is required for the change, and the lapse of time between the two distinct forms of experience is ideally longer rather than shorter.

Again, Wordsworth's doctrine is not false merely because it assumed with him the dignity of a dogma. In the grip of a strong emotion we are never able to control it, much less to give it objective expression in a work of art. Wordsworth was right in holding that, if the artist proposes to make use of his own sensations and emotions, he must allow for an interval between the simple idea and the creative act.

At many points Marcel Proust retraveled at a later time the road down which Wordsworth had pioneered. We find in both the same preoccupation with the past, the same confidence that it holds the secret of the elusive present. The artist is one who can first identify and then later recover the all-important

> spots of time,
> Which with distinct pre-eminence retain
> A vivifying Virtue.

A critical comparison of the two men, their aims and methods, would be interesting. Proust might prove an interpreter of Wordsworth, and Wordsworth might throw much light on Proust. There is, however, one difference between them, — Wordsworth did not need the recurrence of a sensation identical with that experienced at some past time to kindle his imagination. His imagination rolled up like a cloud in a mountain valley from the independent activities of reverie. Proust on the other hand required the identical sight, sound, taste, odor — or one so like it that an identity was suggested — to recover his past life and to find an eternal quality in the world of change. Save for this distinction between the two men, their interests and purposes have much in common. The key experiences which Proust employs were not at the first matters of scrupulous notice. More often than otherwise they had formed no part of constant memory; they were suddenly called up from the realm of forgotten things into consciousness by some sensation which was vaguely recognized as a recurrence of the past. It often took Proust a long time to identify the past moment thus repeated. But in no case is there any suggestion that the experiences which he was eventually to employ had been originally invited as source-material for subsequent authorship. This must be true, also, of all those early experiences of which Wordsworth made such good use. The self-conscious poet was dependent upon the unself-conscious child. Both men insist strongly on the necessity of an "absence" in time as one of the conditions for their art.

Two final points in Wordsworth's theory of poetry should be mentioned. The psychology of association, as he employed it, laid stress upon the mechanical structure of our trains of imagery. Thought must be left undirected to go its necessitated way. Now a wise passiveness may be valid in the arts as a preliminary mental discipline, but there is a point beyond which such passiveness is dangerous. Imagination, as Wordsworth construed and employed it, was an energy arrived at and released by the automatic association of ideas. It was mechanically conceived and mechanically produced. One can only say that, while imagination is never subject to our times and seasons, neither can it be guaranteed by any psychological apparatus. Clearly Wordsworth placed undue confidence in the mechanism which he had from Hartley and Alison as a reliable generator of imagination.

Finally there is the ominous conviction, vouched for by his sources, that the imagination is not immortal, but must pass away. Its loss is to be compensated for by moral sentiments — "criticisms of life," in Arnold's meaning of the term. One reads, in Hartley and Alison, the sentence of death passed upon the imagination, with a sinking heart. Neither Hartley nor Alison had much imagination and, therefore, they were not involved in the consequences of their carefree Jeremiad. With Wordsworth it was otherwise. If he had received at their hands his gift of poetic life, he received also advance notice of his poetic death. The adventure on which he embarked was, as his sources described it, one which must be in the order of nature fatal for his art. The system assured him that he was to outlive his own creative powers. That apprehension, voiced constantly in his verse, darkens all of Wordsworth's joys and becomes in the ode on the *Intimations of Immortality* the last great issue of his life. The *Ode* is a conscious farewell to his art, a dirge sung over his departing powers. The pity of it is that he died, or consented to his poetic death, merely because a doctrinaire psychology required it. He had kept the faith to the end and was self-immolated on the altar of his system. At this point Wordsworth's career rises to the height of genuine tragedy. The psychological scriptures must be fulfilled. The things concerning him must have an end. The prophecy about the mortality of the imagination written by Hartley and Alison was accomplished in Wordsworth.

Let us hear the conclusion of the matter. We have in Wordsworth a poet restricted by his theories of art within very narrow limits. He is denied classicism, at least consciously. He is self-exiled from both epic and dramatic themes. He is confined to the simplest subjects in order to make sure of primal emotions and ideas. He is, in so far as his poems are to be autobiographical, remanded to his own past and required to look with suspicion upon present joys. And for the composition of verse he is supposed ideally to allow a lapse of many years between some early sense experience and the final act of poetic creation. If in his later years Wordsworth was driven to make present joys the matter of his song, he must have felt that in so doing he was taking a risk.

Critics have never tired of laboring Wordsworth's departures from his system. They tell us that we need not take seriously an apparatus which in practice the poet himself treated cavalierly. In minor matters of diction Wordsworth's later usage was modified. But in the poems by which he is remembered and for which he will always be read he worked in sight of his system and with an eye fixed steadily upon it. He cannot be understood, and it is even doubtful whether he can be properly appreciated, in want of his baggage train. But what is far more to our immediate purpose, the system accounts for the anti-climax.

A little reflection on Wordsworth's situation at some time about 1806 or 1807 will suggest the difficulty in which he found himself. The permutations and combinations of his restricted subjects — the local aspects of nature and the undiversified lives of his dalesmen in Westmorland — were by that time thoroughly explored, if not exhausted. Thereafter, as Jeffrey intimated, he tended to become an imitator of his past self; a dangerous situation, since imitation is not creation. During the golden decade he had used his best material with prodigality. The first books of *The Prelude* incorporated the matchless little poems about rowing and nutting and skating which were no small part of his most precious heritage from the past. These remembered sensations of childhood were, in Jeffrey's phrase, "the capital of the concern." Once this patrimony from the child, who was the father of the man, had been spent, there was nothing to replace it. Ten years of consistent work must have used up all the emotionally charged memories from infancy and boyhood, which provided him, according to his theory of the genesis of poems, with his most serviceable themes.

We may say, True, Wordsworth drew on his initial store of subject matter prodigally, even recklessly, but surely he should have been able to re-stock his mind and heart with fresh source-material for further verse. The idea is not original with us. The same thought crossed his mind in 1798 at Tintern:

> And now, with gleams of half extinguished thought,
> With many recognitions dim and faint,
> And somewhat of a sad perplexity,
> The picture of the mind revives again:
> While here I stand, not only with the sense
> Of present pleasure, but with pleasing thoughts
> That in this moment there is life and food
> For future years.

Anyone who understands how the human mind works knows that any such conscious and deliberate quest for experience must be self-defeating. If you can say, "I am now having a most important experience," your ability to use such words denies your experience the importance you would impute to it. You cannot stage-manage or superintend the history of simple emotions and ideas in any such manner. Wordsworth was sincere in the self-congratulation of that moment, but he was none the less in error. The convert to Hartley and Alison, the author with an eye squinted to his professional future, was no longer the wild and carefree boy who had rowed and skated on the lake, who had pillaged the nut trees, and who had hooted his mimicry at the owls across the valley. Mr. Fausset detects the flaw in the lines; he errs only in construing them as conscious hypocrisy.

Wordsworth discovered the truth slowly and admitted it grudgingly. The concession is finally made in the reflective *Intimations of Immortality*. By 1806 he knew that the hope expressed so confidently on the Wye in 1798 was never to be realized. With the end of the golden decade he felt the "prison house" begin to close around him. Given his theory of the genesis of poetry, given his own greatest poems in vindication of the theory, we cannot see any alternative. If poetry may be written only in this manner, every poet is faced with the certain prospect of a dismal anti-climax. Wordsworth, as has been pointed out, is not the only poet who followed this logic to its end. Leopardi's life and work, by his own confession, marched side by side with Wordsworth's. And if we discern similar anti-climaxes among minor poets who have practised poetry after this kind, their sorry aftermaths are less poignant than Wordsworth's only because they lacked his initial single-mindedness and his authentic genius.

I am persuaded, therefore, that Wordsworth's decline was a foredoomed conclusion to his life as a poet, given his technical premises and the restricted subjects which were his patrimony from the earlier years of simple sensations and ideas. We may date the advent of the anti-climax when we will; the date does not matter. His capital was sunk in a concern which by its own articles of incorporation was destined to go bankrupt.

There are few bits of forthright narrative in Wordsworth more moving than the lines in the sixth book of *The Prelude* which tell the story of the crossing of the Alps. The peasant whom they questioned at the head of the pass said

> thatt henceforward all our course
> Was downwards, with the current of that Stream.
> Hard of belief, we question'd him again,
> And all the answers which the Man return'd
> To our inquiries, in their sense and substance,
> Translated by the feelings which we had
> Ended in this; *that we had crossed the Alps.*

In one form or another the idea is written very deeply into Wordsworth, — there is a point beyond which the glory passes away and the path lies downward.

Had Wordsworth's theories of poetry happened to be of quite another kind, had adverse criticism not driven him to such extremes of stubbornness, had his psychology granted him more present joys, had he been a classicist, had he been an epic or dramatic poet, the story might have been different. But then, he would not have been William Wordsworth. Meanwhile, given the man we have, it is conceivable that the earlier and the later poems are two faces of the same shield. If so, the former gain in worth precisely because they had cost so much in prefatory discipline and were to cost so much in their inevitable aftermath.

Wordsworth's poetical history is a comment on the folly of attempting to make a theology do duty as a religion. A theology serves to explain and thus to guarantee to us such religion as we have already experienced. It has, within itself, being retrospective rather than prophetic, no power to guarantee a perpetual renewal of the spiritual life.

II

THE CONDUCT OF LIFE

CHAPTER IX

The Play-Fellow of Fancy

THE inherent limitations of Wordsworth's system brought him, as we have seen, to a dead end. But his point of arrival was like one of the *cirques* in the Pyrenees. A series of truly majestic ideas surrounded him. If the professional adventure had ended in frustration, the personal experience was for him, and must remain for his readers, one of fulfillment.

Modern criticism of the poet, interested in the technical problem, tends to stress the professional defeat. A more generous appreciation must insist upon the joy which Wordsworth knew and which he still spreads "in widest commonalty." When the ordinary traveler has reached Gavarnie, he can go no further. But going there has been a pleasure and reaching there is a sufficient end in itself. His system led Wordsworth to certain views of nature, religion, and the moral struggle which are so characteristic of him that they are almost peculiar to him. In justice to the system, that its profit may be entered against its loss, we should contemplate with him at the end of the professional adventure the unfolded view of nature, man, and God.

Our point of departure is his youthful despondency. From the time that England declared war on France until his settlement at Racedown, — that is, from February, 1793, to September, 1795, — Wordsworth was in a state of grievous distress. We do him a grave injustice if, following Matthew Arnold's lead, we insist on ignoring his

distress. We do him an equal injustice if we come to a
mistaken conclusion about its nature. There is only one
worse error, denial of the distress, an error made by all his
first critics.

The North British Review, commenting on the 1849
edition of the collected poems, says of Wordsworth that
"he appears to have passed through the battle of life un-
wounded." It should be remembered that the judgment
was passed in want of *The Prelude* and was, therefore,
more warranted then than it would have been at any time
after 1850. Yet one would suppose that a sympathetic
reading of the parts of *The Excursion* which deal with
"despondency" and its "correction" might have suggested their autobiographical nature. It was an early
critical convention that the principals of the protracted
conversation in *The Excursion* were merely facets of the
author's own mind. Nevertheless, the reviewer goes
blandly on, perfecting the effigy:

In the life of every man distinguished for what is called intensity of character, there will almost certainly be found some
sore biographical circumstance — some fact deeper and more
momentous than all the rest — some strictly historical source of
melancholy, that must be discovered and investigated, if we
would comprehend his ways. . . . If there be anything specific
and original in his life, this, it would seem, can only be produced
by the operation upon him of some one overbearing accident or
event, that, rousing him to a new wakefulness, and evoking all
that is latent in his nature, shall bind these impressions and convictions in a mass together, breathe through them the stern element of personal concern and impart to them its seal and impression. . . . But Wordsworth, happily for himself, seems to
have met with no such accident of revolution . . . nothing occurred in his journey to strike him down as a dead man, and
agonize him into a full knowledge of the whole mystery of the
present. . . . The ink of Wordsworth is never his own blood.[1]

---

1. *The North British Review*, XIII (1850), 506–507.

The printing of *The Prelude* should have destroyed this lifeless and unlifelike effigy, but twenty-five years had to elapse before Leslie Stephen challenged it, and even his essay made little impression, since Matthew Arnold hastened to repair Stephen's vandalism. *The Prelude* leaves us in no doubt as to the facts. For nearly three years after his return from France at the end of 1792 Wordsworth was in a critical condition, both mentally and emotionally. There are long stretches of days and weeks here of which we have no record, — the only undocumented period of Wordsworth's life. He speaks of himself as one suffering from a "strong disease."

> Most melancholy at that time, O Friend!
> Were my day-thoughts, my dreams were miserable.
>
> Time, since Man first drew breath, has never moved
> With such a weight upon his wings as now.
>
> Sick, wearied out with contrarieties,
> Yielded up moral questions in despair.

His illness, as we have seen, is at present diagnosed as a guilty conscience, attending the mounting certainty that he had forsaken, or was about to forsake, both Annette and France. Some such theory is a possible answer to the riddle of his despondency and, given the present fashion of reducing all mental distress to terms of sexual frustration, is the answer most likely to appeal to our time. I have indicated certain reservations which must be entered against the hypothesis of a guilt-feeling, now invoked to explain Wordsworth's life and work after 1796.

But if Wordsworth's conscience was not hag-ridden by the memory of Annette, what other account can be given of his distress? The passages in *The Prelude* which describe his misery cannot be inventions. Altogether too much space is given to the themes of restoration and correction to allow us to suppose that there had been no impairment of his powers and no attendant despondency.

Indeed, had the distresses been literary fictions Wordsworth, after the manner of minor pessimistic poets, would have left them unrelieved. The record of his resolute grappling with them is proof of their intimate nature.

Up to the time he left France, in December, 1792, or in January, 1793, Wordsworth had passed through two periods, each quite distinct. As a boy he had lived a healthy life, alert and open to impressions stamped upon his senses by the outer world. The nascent poet had through those years the excess of sensibility which he held to be an initial requisite for the poet's calling. The order of nature lay like a heavy weight upon his senses, and lodged itself deep in memory.

The times of infancy and childhood had been followed, quite normally, by later years of youth in which the world within, his own thoughts and ideas and feelings, achieved an equal intensity. He was pleased with his fancies. The only subject at Cambridge which he found in any way congenial was mathematics:

> Mighty is the charm
> Of those abstractions to a mind beset
> With images, and haunted by itself;
> And specially delightful unto me
> Was that clear Synthesis built up aloft
> So gracefully, even then when it appear'd
> No more than as a playing, or a toy
> Embodied to the sense, not what it is
> In verity, an independent world
> Created out of pure Intelligence.

There is in the whole story of the Cambridge years and the following months in London the suggestion of a youth preoccupied with his own thoughts and wanting in healthful contacts with the outer world. Since we are dealing with one who had the stuff of poetry in him, the second period was as intense and absorbing as the first had been.

By the time he was twenty, therefore, Wordsworth was equipped with two worlds: deep impressions of external

nature registered upon him by one very restricted area of
this earth's face, and inventions of fancy which were independent of objective fact. The latter of these worlds had
not been, when he went to France in 1791, "remanded" —
to use his own term — to the former. Conceivably Wordsworth might have kept the world within in closer contact
with the world without had his years of later youth been
spent in his own home counties. There was nothing in the
Cambridge fenland or on the sky-line of London to suggest
the hills and lakes which in childhood had lain so heavy on
his mind and heart. He confesses his inability to find in
the scenery of the south any suggestion of nature as he had
first felt and known it. His earlier experiences had such
authority that no other scene ever matched for him the
imperiousness of the crags and torrents of his boyhood
home. The highly individualized landscape of the Lake
Country seems to have denied him after childhood perfect
communion with any other aspect of nature and must have
helped to increase, during the Cambridge terms, the London months, and the years in France, his sense of the
mounting reality of the world within, in neglect of the
world without.

Thus far we have a story of the normal unfolding of any
human life. It differs from other lives only in its intensity;
whether as a boy or as a youth there is no slackness of the
strings, — they are taut, and the pitch of life is higher than
is the common lot. The youthful Wordsworth had both
the sensibility and the imagination of a poet, even while
written poetry was still occasional or wholly in abeyance.

The autumn of 1791 found him in France at a time when
the inner world was far more real to him than the outer
world. His enthusiasm for the Revolution was a natural
response to a theory and a program which promised to
bear out his own ideas. There is an entire want of surprise
at the course of events in France and a matter-of-fact
consent to them, almost listless precisely because they

were taken for granted. The bliss and joy of being alive at
the time had their ground in the poet's simple persuasion
that "mild schemers" like himself had now a world near
at hand to confirm "the region of their peaceful selves."
They were about to live, as they supposed,

> Not in Utopia, subterraneous Fields,
> Or some secreted Island, Heaven knows where,
> But in the very world which is the world
> Of all of us, the place in which, in the end
> We find our happiness, or not at all.

We may doubt whether the Wordsworth of the early
1790's had given any serious thought to the structure of
human society. In the summer tramp across France in '90
he had been far more interested in natural scenes than in
political affairs. He returned to France in '91, not as a
conscious recruit to the Revolution, but as a young man
bent on getting up his French, in the hope of finding a job
as tutor back in England. The year 1792 involved him
more and more in the affairs of the Revolution — though
his Girondist connections were of a milder manner than
the times eventually allowed — and we need not doubt the
sincerity of his republican protestations. Yet there was no
bloodshed and a good deal of day-dreaming in his republicanism, prolonging the tempers which had been dominant
over all the preceding years. As 1792 wore on there was
much that disquieted him. The extremer party "were
strong through their impiety," yet Wordsworth held to his
conviction that "nothing hath a natural right to last but
equity and reason," and he was without "the least fear
about the end of things." His return to England was
"compell'd by nothing less than absolute want of funds."
No one seriously questions his blunt statement. Common
decency, which he never wanted, forced him to plan for the
support of Annette and her child. Even the most unsym-
pathetic modern critics do not charge him with consciously
deserting in 1793 either the mistress or the cause. Al-

though somewhat disturbed by the turn that public affairs were taking in France, Wordsworth back in England was still a loyal lover and a confident idealist.

His troubles began with England's declaration of war on France, February 11, 1793. His account of the effect of this event on him is explicit and unequivocal:

Change and subversion from this hour. No shock
Given to my moral nature had I known
Down to that very moment; neither lapse
Nor turn of sentiment that might be nam'd
A revolution, save at this one time,
All else was progress on the self-same path
On which with a diversity of pace
I had been travelling; this a stride at once
Into another region. . . .
                                        I felt
The ravage of this most unnatural strife
In my own heart; there lay it like a weight
At enmity with all the tenderest springs
Of my enjoyments.

I see no reason to doubt his statement. Although the war had an added poignancy because it came between him and Annette, this was not his first or greatest grievance. He was outraged that England had turned against him. It is difficult to understand what other course he could have expected of his country, since France had already declared war on England ten days earlier. But his political sympathies were still across the channel.

The next eighteen months were passed in a vagrant way, more or less seditious in their companionships. There was a lonely time on Salisbury Plain, a walking tour in Wales with the first visit to the Wye, a trip to the north to see Dorothy, and in Joseph Johnson's shop in London much wild talk with Paine, Horne Tooke, and Godwin. During these years *Guilt and Sorrow*, already in embryo as *The Female Vagrant*, was completed, and *The Borderers* was conceived, though it was finished only after the settlement

at Racedown. The poems of the period both conceal and
reveal Wordsworth's thoughts and feelings. We may not
press them too closely for autobiographical detail, yet in
their mood and substance they were faithful to their
author's temper. It is not a happy mind or an easy heart
that we meet:

> A Man by pain and thought compelled to live,
> Yet loathing life.

> From the sweet thoughts of home
> And from all hope I was forever hurled.

> Homeless near a thousand homes I stood.

> Of Time's sure help to calm and reconcile,
> Joy's second spring and Hope's long-treasured smile,
> 'Twas not for *him* to speak — a man so tried.

We have here reliable source-material. *The Prelude*, written retrospectively, confirms the contemporary evidence.
For two or three years Wordsworth was haunted by

> a sense,
> Of treachery and desertion in the place
> The holiest that I knew of, my own soul.

The nature of his strong disease is plain. The outer
world would no longer come to heel at the command of the
mind. The operations of pure intelligence were being denied by the course of history: first, by the English declaration of war on France and, subsequently, by the degenera-
tion of the Revolution into a tyranny. Professor Beatty
bows in passing to this explanation of the poet's distress
and dismisses it as "juvenile inexperience," an ignorance
of the truth that hard facts and Utopian theories seldom
coincide. The phrase "juvenile inexperience" is unfortunate. It carries with it a sophisticated suggestion that
facts and ideas should not be expected to agree. That they
by no means do so is a discovery which may be made in
our juvenile years; but, once made, the discovery should

continue to distress us to the day of our death. The two worlds ought to fit each other better than they do. The attempt to arrive at some resolution of the riddle is the substance of all philosophy and of all religion.

To be sure, Wordsworth was an inexpert and juvenile person, when confronted at the age of twenty-three with the discrepancy between the world within and the world without. But had he not faced the problem then in the terms of political thinking, he would certainly have had to make his reckoning with it in other terms at some later time. He differs from most men only in this, that once having seen the issue he could not put it aside. He cared passionately, savagely, at the time, and he never ceased to care, that the world of fact falls short of the ideal world. To the last his "juvenile inexperience" refused to make its peace with cynicism, and in the refusal we discover his most distinguishing trait as a thinker. Therefore, when he speaks of "a sense of treachery and desertion" in his own soul, it was not his soul that had deserted either itself or the world, but the world that had deserted his soul. He indicts the history of the time for failing to vindicate his idealism. So far from admitting guilt to himself, he bitterly condemned events which at the critical moment had betrayed him.

His major grievance was an intellectual one. It is difficult for persons to whom the life of the mind is not paramount to understand how a man can entertain such a grievance and suffer deeply from such a cause. But we are not dealing here with a man to whom his thoughts did not matter. We are dealing with a man for whom the mind was life's "main region," and at a time in his life when the independent creations of pure intelligence were assumed to be truths sure of confirmation from the world without. Life, as Wordsworth knew it and cared for it, had stopped.

In his surprise and indignation Wordsworth was running true to form. He had, I think, a certain measure of generous concern for France. He was sorry to see its aims miscarry and its hopes wrecked. Nevertheless, the French debacle was not what pained him most. His greatest pain was intimate and, if you will, selfish in its nature. His blame of history had to be reconstrued as an adverse judgment on himself. The inference was obvious, and pride could not help him to avoid it. He, William Wordsworth, had been shown up as a fool. He knew nothing about reality. His thinking was to no purpose. The order of the universe did not conform to his private imaginings. Wordsworth was always self-centered and never more so than in the first bitter hour when the issue was put to him in terms so plain that he could not deny them. It was Wordsworth *contra mundum*, and the world had much the best of the first skirmish.

If any proof of the foregoing argument is needed we have it in the lines,

> in the process I began to feel
> That, if the emancipation of the world
> Were missed, I should at least secure my own
> And be in part compensated.

These are not the words of an impulsive and generous nature. No passionate patriot or revolutionary could have written them. For such persons the defeat of the cause is also the loss of all personal life worth the name. Although Wordsworth does not appraise his own emancipation as of equal value with that of the world, the mention of both in a single breath gives us a clue to his character. The Wordsworth so disclosed is not a wholly admirable person; he lacks here, as at certain other points which we have cited, selflessness. He was always observing the influence of the world on himself, and recording his resultant states of mind and feeling. His presumption in thinking of his private gains as in any way offsetting the world's failure to win its freedom is almost incredible. The disparity is too great to allow such a comparison. Nevertheless, Wordsworth's ability to think and write the lines is proof that, even in his dealings with the Revolution, he was a poet, not a soldier or a statesman. And as a poet he was right. For a poet writing about a revolution is concerned, not so much with the fortunes of the revolution, as with his own impressions of the event and his reaction to it. The passage is an indication that Wordsworth's distress during those hard years was an intellectual perplexity, not a political disappointment.

What could he hope to get, what did he get, from Godwin? Professor Beatty says that under Godwin's tutelage Wordsworth turned from man as he is to man as he ought to be. The statement is very misleading. Wordsworth up to 1793 had never known man as he is; it is doubtful if he ever knew that man. The only man whom Wordsworth had known was man as he ought to be, and under Godwin's guidance he went farther down that road until the ideal evaporated for want of warrant in fact.

Meanwhile, in the process of outgrowing Godwinism, Wordsworth laid hold of two or three ideas which for the moment seemed to help him. He found in the doctrine of ethical opposites, the issue of good and evil causes in antithetical effects, a temporary explanation of the course of the Revolution. Good men, with the best intent, achieve bad ends because of an element of paradox in the moral order. Furthermore, he was encouraged for a year or so to view whatever happened in England and France with patrician contempt. Godwin affected an aristocracy of intellect which he did not possess, and sought to look down like a passionless deity upon the chances and changes of this mortal world. At the time when Godwin's doctrines first came over his horizon Wordsworth's intellectual self-confidence was imperiled. He wished reassurance about the validity of the operations of the independent intellect and the worth of its creations. He clutched Godwin like a drowning man. Here was a teacher who should save him.

Godwin helped Wordsworth understand his affair with Annette. Professor de Selincourt doubts whether Wordsworth was aware, at the time, of a cooling ardor for his mistress or foresaw his desertion of her. He thinks that up to the end of the year 1795 the poet intended to go back and marry her. The more modern theory that the enthusiasm for Godwin was a deliberate tampering with conscience, an attempt to cauterize remorse, must be read into the poems. Yet the affair, as Wordsworth looked back on it in 1794 or 1795, must have seemed hasty and ill-advised. Why had he done it? Godwin's doctrine of necessity, which made larger room for sexual vagaries than could be found within the conventions, must have been a welcome opiate.

But the love affair was not the source of the real distress. The trouble was that fancy and fact had failed to coincide. Godwin encouraged Wordsworth to go on trying to coerce the world without into conformity to the world within. Wordsworth, with his uncritical and loyal devotion to chosen masters, trusted Godwinism far beyond its deserts. Failing to coerce the facts he fell back upon the central defenses of Godwinism and tried to live in patrician indifference to events, as one whose mind was sufficient to itself. He failed in his endeavor. He had not in him the stuff of absolute idealism. The aggression of the outer world upon his senses in childhood and in early youth had been too strong to be forgotten. Godwin's bleak rationalism seemed to Wordsworth, as he lived with it, pride rather than the truth.

If we consult the books of *The Excursion* which describe the Solitary, we see a picture of Wordsworth as he might have been had his inner history been arrested in 1794 or 1795. The Solitary is the poet's memory of his own state of mind at the height of his Godwinian enthusiasm. In retrospect he seems to himself to have been one sustained by "a proud and most presumptuous confidence," one who gave "a festal air to self-importance," one "galled by pride," "a forward youth" victimized by "rules of inexperienced judgment," and feeding upon "the golden fruit of self-esteem."

The stock deserted-mother theme occurs in a modified form in the description of the Solitary, who had lost first his children and then his sorrowing wife. Yet the passage describing this phase of the Solitary's history is unconvincing. A manufacturer of blank verse, not a poet-lover, wrote the lines,

> My tender Mate became
> The thankful captive of maternal bonds.

The children and their mother are only stage-properties introduced to heighten the Solitary's distress. If Wordsworth had really grieved at the loss of Annette and Caroline, he had thoroughly disguised the fact to himself by 1814. *The Excursion*, as Jeffrey says, abounds in "choice obituaries," and the Solitary's wife and children come under this lifeless category; they have no flesh and blood. But, when he turns to the description of the Solitary's state of mind, Wordsworth becomes, if not poetic, at least convincing. He is writing here of something he had known and felt. The perspective given to the Solitary's affairs is in all probability an accurate account of the relative importance, to the Wordsworth of 1793–95, of Annette on the one hand and his own mental frustration on the other hand. He does not delete the deserted-wife motif, but it is not his main theme.

The Prelude is ten years nearer the facts than is *The Excursion*. Its last three books deal with "Imagination, How Impaired and Restored." Imagination was Wordsworth's name for the mind's initiative, its ability either to create independent worlds or to recreate the world of fact after its heart's desire. His imaginative powers had been impaired by the course of history and had to be restored if

life were to be worth living. The three books in question
give us Wordsworth's account, written long after the
event, of his recourse to Godwinism and his disillusionment with it. His condemnation of Godwinism is, by inference, a condemnation of the concluded second period of
his life, the years which had been given over to

> The careless stillness of a thinking mind
> Self-occupied; to which all outward things
> Are like an idle matter.

The last books of *The Prelude* tell us what happens to a
mind so employed. Protracted speculation carried on without reference to fact becomes a progressive persuasion of
the unreality of life. That way lies madness, and the man
who goes that way eventually reaches the boundary-line
between sanity and insanity. There are in the relevant
passages of *The Prelude* certain references which we can
describe only as intimations of mental instability. Wordsworth was no stranger to the horror of a world within
which is unreal, but his ability to recognize its unreality is
a pledge that he never crossed the border.

Looking back on the idealistic period of his history,
1787 to 1795, — the years from his going up to Cambridge
until his settlement at Racedown, — when his thinking
mind had been self-occupied and when outward things
were idle matters, Wordsworth says with bitterness that
by its end he had become a "Play-fellow of Fancy." Fancy
was, to him, the energy of a mind engaged in aimless invention without salutary reference to the external world. In
retrospect all his miseries seemed to him to have had their
origin in his mental divorce from the outer world. No man,
he seems to say, may safely allow himself to become a
"play-fellow of fancy," though this is a state into which he
may lapse with the best of intentions. Such a person loses
his peace of mind and eventually passes beyond the reasonable order of things into a world where thought is futile

and ultimately suicidal. To quote a modern philosopher, "in the isolated dungeon of his self-consciousness he rots away, unheeded and alone."

Wordsworth's experience is not common. The ruck of men do not care passionately for ideas, or take the life of the mind so seriously. But the case is not without modern parallels, and one could find among convinced pacifists suddenly confronted with August, 1914, suggestive counterparts; idealists who were driven by the brutal irrationality of a world war, first to an attempt to get "above the battle," and then, as facts refused to be stared out of countenance, to cynicism and despair. Wordsworth, to be understood, should be re-read in the terms of the doctrinaire pacifism of the great war. The mental suffering of the type can be very great and of such intensity that it obliterates all other lesser pains.

Mr. Fausset stresses Wordsworth's self-righteousness through all these years and the hypocrisy into which the self-righteousness finally crystallized. He is thinking of Annette. But if Wordsworth's disease was, as I believe it to have been, an intellectual distress, then he became a penitent *par excellence*, who lived to deplore his unhealthy divorce from the actual world. He had played the prodigal with his mind, and he admitted it.

The eleventh and twelfth books of *The Prelude* are little more than a confessional-box, thrown open to the world, with William Wordsworth a spectacle for the gaping multitude. He is in these passages a flagellant scourging himself with savage phrases in condemnation of his "fallacious hopes, vain conceits, benighted mind, sanguine schemes, false philosophy." It is nard to see what further public confession could be expected of him, and in the light of his pitiless self-condemnation it is hard to concede modern criticism the self-righteousness with which it would invest the poet. Few men have ever spoken more ruthlessly of their lapses than Wordsworth in this reflective account of

his "degradations," "presumptions," "bigotries," and
"idolatries." He goes as far as the sacrament of penance
requires and much farther than prudent decencies suggest.
Even so late as the years 1804–05 when *The Prelude* was
being concluded in first draft, his vehemence in self-criti-
cism is an indication that he still felt the need of fortifying
himself against a similar lapse in the future. He had not
yet achieved, indeed he never achieved, immunity to his
strong disease.

The most significant passage, dealing with this whole
period of Wordsworth's life, the initial impairment of his
mental health and its subsequent restoration, is that which
concludes the *Lines Left upon the Seat of a Yew-tree*. The
poem, written in 1795, marks at once Wordsworth's de-
liverance from the spell of Godwin and his returning peace
of mind.

> If Thou be one whose heart the holy forms
> Of young imagination have kept pure,
> Stranger! henceforth be warned; and know that pride,
> Howe'er disguised in its own majesty,
> Is littleness; that he who feels contempt
> For any living thing, hath faculties
> Which he has never used; that thought with him
> Is in its infancy. The man whose eye
> Is ever on himself doth look on one
> The least of Nature's works, one who might move
> The wise man to that scorn which wisdom holds
> Unlawful, ever. O be wiser, Thou!
> Instructed that true knowledge leads to love;
> True dignity abides with him alone
> Who, in the silent hour of inward thought,
> Can still suspect, and still revere himself,
> In lowliness of heart.

I do not see how Wordsworth could have described his
experience more explicitly. He repudiates thought carried
on without love, that is, without reference to a stable object, and thought carried on in arrogant indifference to
fact. He repents of the whole introverted, introspective

life which he had been living for the previous seven or eight years. He had learned, at a heavy price, to suspect himself as a thinker, and the salutary suspicion never left him.

The disease left its mark on Wordsworth. There runs through all his poetry thereafter a shrinking from submitting his ideas to the verification of fact. He dreads to see new places lest they fall short of his expectation, and because, in the very nature of the case, they deprive him of mental pictures which he had already created out of "pure intelligence." The poems recording his travels abroad reflect his dread:

> That day we first
> Beheld the summit of Mont Blanc, and griev'd
> To have a soulless image on the eye
> Which had usurp'd upon a living thought
> That never more could be.

And if, as he says a few lines later, he was eventually "reconciled to realities," the act of reconciliation was not one to which he looked forward with pleasure. It opened the old wound, and stirred the first sharp pain of the most difficult years of his life. The *locus classicus* for this characteristic mental trait of the mature poet is the Yarrow poems. Despite his protestations to the contrary, William Wordsworth preferred Yarrow unvisited to Yarrow visited.

> Be Yarrow stream unseen, unknown!
> It must be, or we shall rue it:
> We have a vision of our own;
> Ah! why should we undo it?

There speaks the impenitent Wordsworth of the revolutionary years. Were he able to stay away from Yarrow for a lifetime, he would prefer it so. Yet there is a necessity, a fatality in things, which compels him to visit and revisit Yarrow. He does his best to persuade himself that Yarrow in fact is better than Yarrow in fancy, but he never quite succeeds.

To the degree that he was cured of this ill, which had been all but fatal to his mental powers, Wordsworth owed his cure to a return to nature. Citing his own experience, he once wrote to "Mathetes" that when a young man finds himself the victim of an excessive subjectivity, he should "be remanded to nature." Some kind of saving contact must be established with the outer world, and nature is our most obvious resort in such a time of need. We should remember, therefore, that in reading what Wordsworth has to say of the world around us — its familiar sights and sounds — we are not reading "nature poetry." We are handling a medicine of the soul, elements which had for him the energy of a sacramental grace bestowing salvation from the presumptuous sins of the independent intellect.

CHAPTER X

Nature

IN THE fifth chapter of his *Apologia* Cardinal Newman says of his entry into the Church of Rome, "It was like coming into port after a rough sea." He was once asked to give in a few words his reasons for going over to Rome. He refused. He said that he could hope to make his course plain only to those persons who were willing to live through with him, patiently and at length, the many years prior to the final step taken in 1845.

Wordsworth's retreat to the Lake District "was like coming into port after a rough sea." If he had been asked to tell in a few words his reasons for beginning to write in 1797 simple poems about natural objects, he would have replied in words not unlike Newman's. His choice of subjects is intelligible only to those who are willing to live through with him in detail the time of painful perplexity which had preceded his return to the countryside. Even so transparent a poem as *The Daffodils* cannot be felt with anything like its original intensity save by a tedious approach through the years from his entrance to Cambridge until his settlement at Racedown.

There are four lines of Emily Dickinson's which throw some light on Wordsworth's history. They are the lines by which she is best known.

> Adventure most unto itself
> The Soul condemned to be;
> Attended by a Single Hound —
> Its own Identity.[1]

---

1. Martha Dickinson Bianchi and Alfred Leete Hampson, *The Poems of Emily Dickinson*, Centenary Edition (Boston: Little, Brown & Company, 1930), p. 223. By permission of the publisher.

Poetry requires of him who would write it a strong persuasion of his integrity. Poetry cannot be had from persons who have forfeited and failed to recover their identity. The imaginative act is one which attempts to unify the world with which it deals, and, since this unity is created rather than observed, a divided nature cannot impute to outward things a quality which it lacks. There must be in the poet an area of "central peace." Emily uses the vivid metaphor of a hound at heel to picture her reassurance at this vital point.

Wordsworth's "single hound" had, by the middle of the year 1795, all but slipped its leash. His mind, as his Godwin interlude drew to its futile conclusion, can have been little more than the remembrance of things past, lying in disorder and confusion. In the first book of *The Prelude* he tells us that the backward glance discovered "discordant elements . . . terrors, pains, and early miseries, regrets, vexations, lassitudes interfused." He is not a pessimistic philosopher laying on dark colors with an eye to the effect; he is a faithful witness to the felt discontinuity of his early life. He was farmed out at school in Hawkshead, housed casually in his vacations, sent on to Cambridge, and graduated. He tramped in France and Switzerland and Italy, he idled in London, he turned up now and then at the house of a relative, but seems never to have been welcome anywhere. He spent a year and a half on the Loire under conditions which were alien and unsettling. He returned to England to find himself at cross-purposes with his native land, he kept furtive trysts with likeminded malcontents, he was a lonely vagrant on bleak plains and in wild valleys. Finally he was buried in the deep country to resume his life and to get on with his vocation as best he could. It is quite apparent that, when he consulted memory, Wordsworth found it hard to harmonize the "discordant elements" which it provided.

No man in that state is well advised to press further into

the dark cave of subjectivity. The guarantee of the integrity of his life must be had by reference to some shrine of constancy in the world outside. There are, in the outer world, two types of fact to which a man needing such reassurance may turn, — permanent human institutions and the order of inanimate nature. Burke, for example, had he ever doubted his own identity, could have reassured himself by appealing to the history of England and by recalling his citizenship in the English state. Newman, after his submission to Rome, can never have doubted his integrity; his inviolate soul was guaranteed to him by that society. Church and state serve many men in such stead at the times when their inner life lacks continuity and coherence.

Under other circumstances Wordsworth might have appealed, in 1795, to his identification with church and state. But at that time he had yet to be reconverted to Anglicanism. As for England, it was another five years before he rediscovered her and, in the face of Napoleon's rise, felt her blood running in his veins. For the moment the men and movements he knew best were as confused as his own experience had been. Indeed, the incoherence of his life had arisen from his participation with them in confusions worse confounded. Thus he speaks of "the mean and vulgar works of Man," "rash judgments, sneers of selfish men," "impatient or fallacious hopes," "heat of passion, excessive zeal, vain conceits." He had not merely observed these defects in other men; he had been party to them, and had tasted their bitter dregs at the bottom of his cup of heady idealism. The unstable causes with which Wordsworth had been identified provided, therefore, no constant fact by which he might reaffirm the unimpaired integrity of his personal life.

For this reason he turned to "the permanent forms of nature." We should never forget, in reading Wordsworth's nature poetry, that here as elsewhere his own mind is the "haunt and main region of his song." The subjective interest can always be identified beneath the veneer provided by natural objects. So, for example, in the familiar poem about the rainbow:

> My heart leaps up when I behold
> A rainbow in the sky:
> So was it when my life began;
> So is it now I am a man;
> So be it when I shall grow old,
> Or let me die!
> The Child is father of the Man;
> And I could wish my days to be
> Bound each to each by natural piety.

The lines are plainly not about a rainbow. They are not even an elaboration of Wordsworth's doctrine of the pre-eminence of childhood, though they contain what is perhaps his most familiar line on the subject. The poem is a study of the soul's identity, and might very properly bear Emily's caption, *The Single Hound*. "Natural piety," as Wordsworth here conceives it, is little more than reassurance, partly psychological and partly ethical, that the "discordant elements" of his self-consciousness can be reconciled; that life has continuity, coherence, and unity. The rainbow came to his rescue when he doubted whether he was William Wordsworth.

If Wordsworth was a nature mystic, a designation very commonly accorded him, he was a twice-born rather than a once-born mystic. As a child he had been in direct and unreflective contact with nature. Then the outer "props of his affections" [1] had been withdrawn, and his life had been lived in his own thoughts. These had issued in futility, divorced from the world without, and in maturity he

---

1. Legouis and other commentators on *The Prelude* have construed the passage in the second book, which speaks of the removal of the props of affection as a reference to the death, first of his mother, and then of his father. Clearly, the reference is to a waning dependence upon sense impressions of the outer world.

came back again to nature to recover the substance, reality, unity of his inner life. Matthew Arnold's lines,

> He laid us as we lay at birth
> On the cool flowery lap of earth,

have the right ring because they go on to admit that souls so laid have previously been dead and dried up. Arnold concedes in his elegy an element in Wordsworth's poetry which the essay of 1879 ignores, the truth that the ease which Wordsworth gives us, as he lays us on the lap of earth, can be fully felt only by those whose wounded human spirits have turned elsewhere upon beds of pain.

As we toil through the closing books of *The Prelude*, which retell the story of his most troubled years and bring it to an end, we happen here and there upon stray passages from the authentic Wordsworth. As Coleridge said of such lines, were we to find them in the desert, we should recognize them at once and should shout, "Wordsworth!" So, for example,

> the wind and sleety rain
> And all the business of the elements,
> The single sheep, and the one blasted tree,
> And the bleak music of that old stone wall.

The lapse of years has not effaced from that quatrain its author's hallmark, nor has studied imitation ever duplicated the original. In this area "others abide our question," Wordsworth is free.

The differentia of such a passage is reasonably plain, and may be indicated by a parallel. The closing chapters of the Book of Job, particularly Chapter XXXVIII, give us what is perhaps the classic account, in our tradition, of the natural world as it is busied with its own affairs and as it exists in its own right. Browning asks, in another connection, "Has it your vote to be so, if it can?" The natural world, as Job conceives it in his concluding chapters, is not liable or even amenable to such a question, since it is pre-

sented as existing quite apart from human suffrage. The
Book of Job ends by confronting us with "rain on the
earth, where no man is; on the wilderness wherein there is
no man." There is not the slightest concession to any
humanism; indeed the passage is marked by an almost
studied inhumanity. The intention of the argument, which
is elaborated by the voice of God, is quite clear. Job is to
understand — his sufferings and perplexities to the contrary — that there is a vast, varied, and joyous world of
things existing independent of him, and that this world
does not require his private sanction in order to go on.

Much of the Wordsworth scene is of this order. There
are waste places, winds, elemental transactions taking
place in indifference to man. It is as though the world of
nature which the poet had neglected was bent, when he
approached it again, on keeping its secrets to itself. It is
all very like the end of Job. For the moment man is ignored in the presence of realities which stand in their own
right. Wordsworth employed more than once, to indicate
the processes of nature, the prosaic term "goings-on." In
one instance, at least, he deleted it from his verse because
friends persuaded him that it carried his theory of poetic
diction to an unwarranted extreme. Yet those words ex-
press "how he felt" about nature, even though they may
not define "what he felt." Re-read the lines describing the
descent of the Italian side of the Simplon:

> The immeasurable height
> Of woods decaying, never to be decay'd,
> The stationary blasts of water-falls,
> And everywhere along the hollow rent
> Winds thwarting winds, bewilder'd and forlorn,
> The torrents shooting from the clear blue sky,
> The rocks that mutter'd close upon our ears,
> Black drizzling crags that spake by the way-side
> As if a voice were in them, the sick sight
> And giddy prospect of the raving stream,
> The unfetter'd clouds, and region of the Heavens,

Tumult and peace, the darkness and the light
Were all like workings of one mind, the features
Of the same face, blossoms upon one tree,
Characters of the great Apocalypse,
The types and symbols of Eternity,
Of first, and last, and midst, and without end.

In such a passage, as in the lines about "the wind and sleety rain," one meets the indubitable Wordsworth. He seems truer to himself in this field than in any other, and even his poems about the simplest human subjects are corollaries of this major mood and manner. *The Prelude* comes instantly and imperiously alive at such moments, and its prosy reaches are the more dreary for the contrast. In the latter area Wordsworth's mind is felt to be laboring, in the former it is free, exultant, and powerful with an energy not unlike that of the universe itself.

For the sake of coming again and again upon the surprise and majesty of so much of Wordsworth's poetry as discovers to us the elemental "goings-on" of nature, we are willing to pay the high initial price of toiling through with the poet the steps that led him back to her. Here, in the result, are imperious motions of the human mind, unmatched in modern times and only in the rarest instances equalled in any elder time. The achieved control of the English language, which is a stubborn medium; the will-to-power over words exercising itself with the utmost ease; the sweep of vision and the integrity of an emotion which cannot be successfully feigned; the highly individualized style, which may be parodied but never imitated; — these are the marks of Wordsworth when in maturity he was remanded to nature and

> In Nature's presence stood . . .
> A sensitive, and a creative soul.

Wordsworth was to recreate nature by his poetic imagination, but the natural world with which he was to deal thereafter had for him, when in maturity he returned to it, an imperious and majestic reality of its own. Therein lay its initial meaning for him and its power to serve him in his need. If, at that time, he had not approached rocks, stones, and trees in the spirit of the closing chapters of the Book of Job, the natural order could not have given him the assurance he required. Had nature been dependent upon his suffrage for its life it would have been at once involved with those "discordant elements" of his thought and feeling, which he was seeking to bring into intelligible sequence and order. Like most of Wordsworth's victories, the victory over excessive introspection was hard won, and its fruits were precarious. He never dared to withdraw all his troops from the conquered but unsubjugated area. Had he been certain of his unassailable identity he would not have found it necessary to reassure himself that when he grew old the rainbow would still be in the sky to guarantee him that identity. Wordsworth is never more human than in the intimations that his mature faith was always held in the face of residual doubt.

Nature, then, was to him, as he came to the golden decade, his one sure witness to "enduring things." He was, however, unable to conceive of the external world as dead matter void of a principle or process akin to thought. There is in the fourth book of *The Prelude* the strange passage describing the dream about the Arab with his two books, Euclid's *Elements* and a prophecy of the end of the world. Waking from his dream the poet reflects on it:

> A thought is with me sometimes, and I say,
> Should earth by inward throes be wrench'd throughout,
> Or fire be sent from far to wither all
> Her pleasant habitations, and dry up
> Old Ocean in his bed left sing'd and bare,
> Yet would the living Presence still subsist
> Victorious; and composure would ensue,
> And kindlings like the morning; presage sure,
> Though slow, perhaps, of a returning day.

In the same spirit the Wanderer looks out over the natural
scene, to say,

> Some shadowy intimations haunt me here,
> That in these shows a chronicle survives
> Of purposes akin to those of Man.

Passages of this type have no suggestion that the "Presence" or "purpose" requires the mind of man for its
operations. If at an earlier time Wordsworth had been
able to think of mathematical abstraction as an "independent world," so at a later time he conceded to the
"Presences of Nature" their free and sovereign state. Yet,
such is the healing paradox of life, that man's thoughts,
though not the sum of all thinking nor perhaps the major
manifestations of the "eternity of thought," are part of
a total thoughtfulness of things.

> And I have felt
> A presence that disturbs me with the joy
> Of elevated thoughts; a sense sublime
> Of something far more deeply interfused,
> Whose dwelling is the light of setting suns,
> And the round ocean and the living air,
> And the blue sky, and in the mind of man.

The lines recall a similar passage from *The Wisdom of
Solomon* (VII: 17–20) in which the author describes the
objects made known to us by wisdom:

> . . . the operation of the elements:
> The beginning, ending, and midst of the times: the alterna-
> tions of the turning of the sun, and the changes of the seasons:
> The circuits of years, and the positions of stars:
> The natures of living creatures, and the furies of wild beasts:
> the violence of winds, and the reasonings of men: the diversities
> of plants, and the virtues of roots.

The "reasonings of men," written into the catalogue,
are but an incident in the sum of things known. Wordsworth's lines in *Tintern Abbey* give us much the same sug-

gestion of relative values. "The mind of man" is only one
of the local habitations of the "Presence," and the passage
seems an anti-climax rather than a climax. When he
wrote *Tintern Abbey* Wordsworth looked more hopefully to
setting suns for a revelation of the "Presence" than to the
mind of man. But with those lines — and they are the
classic statement of an idea which constantly recurs in
Wordsworth — man is readmitted to the world of reality.
What the poet says in praise of our childhood, he says by
inference in defense of our maturity:

> Emphatically such a Being lives.
> An inmate of this *active* universe;
> From nature largely he receives; nor so
> Is satisfied, but largely gives again,
> For feeling has to him imparted strength,
> And powerful in all sentiments of grief,
> Of exultation, fear, and joy, his mind,
> Even as an agent of the one great mind,
> Creates, creator and receiver both.
> Working but in alliance with the works
> Which it beholds. — Such, verily, is the first
> Poetic spirit of our human life.

These passages give us Wordsworth's perspective. The
mind of man is one of the means through which "the one
great Mind" finds expression, and in man that mind is
most properly employed when working in alliance with the
environing universe.[1] The priority in time, the initiative
in experience, and even the greater degree of excellence,
rest with the "Presence" in the outer order. But man is
not, as in the chapter from Job, stubbornly excluded from
nature. Nature is willing to be wooed by poets.

Knowing Wordsworth's earlier history, we might fear
that the concession would prove a leak in the dike,
through which the ebbed tides of introspection could

1.   "Subservient strictly to external things
        With which it commun'd. An auxiliar light
        Came from my mind. . . ."

flood back to inundate his hard-won peace of mind. He
seems consciously to have defended himself against such a
catastrophe by the scrupulousness of his descriptions of
nature. He admits in one of his prefaces that the associative processes of his mind may have led him to attach to
insignificant objects a value which other minds, with different habits of association, did not accord them. He
realized that here and there he might have been absurd.
But he insisted that his "trains of imagery" should always
be censored by a sober realism. Whatever Wordsworth
made of nature, as recreated by his imagination, he was in
the first instance an accurate observer. A writer in *The
Edinburgh Review* (April, 1849) says that poets may be
forgiven false sentiment, false passion, false logic,

but false description is a scandal to the outward senses: and if a
poet plants his willows on the mountain side, or insists upon the
yeomanly oak bathing its unbound tresses in the flowing stream,
— still more should his apples be bold enough to come "before
the swallow dares" and his lambs begin to bleat for a better
shepherd "when rivers rage and rocks grow cold," he may possibly, if not very much in the fashion, fall in with readers who
will object to being deceived with their eyes open.

There is no false description in Wordsworth's nature
poetry. Nature is often transfigured by his imagination,
it is not transformed. The rocky foundation of fact may
be identified beneath the superstructure of the verse. For
this reason Wordsworth's nature poetry has worn well.
The scientific mind may find it at times in excess, but never
in error.

What now of man's place in nature? The eighth book of
The Prelude gives the best answer. The love of nature led
the poet in his early twenties to a love of man. The first
eight books of *The Prelude* remind one of the two opening
chapters of *The Return of the Native*. At the outset of his
story Hardy writes of a universe untenanted by man.

Egdon Heath is a "Face on which Time Makes but Little
Impression." Then, when this world void of men has been
described, "Humanity appears upon the Scene." The
reddleman gazes in the dusk at the sky-line:

> [His] eye finally settled upon one noteworthy object up there.
> It was a barrow. . . . It formed the pole and axis of this heath-
> ery world.
>
> As the resting man looked at the barrow he became aware
> that its summit, hitherto the highest object in the whole prospect
> round, was surmounted by something higher. . . . The first in-
> stinct of an imaginative stranger might have been to suppose it
> the person of one of the Celts who built the barrow, so far had
> all of modern date withdrawn from the scene. It seemed a sort
> of last man among them, musing for a moment before dropping
> into eternal night with the rest of his race.
>
> There the form stood, motionless as the hill beneath. Above
> the plain rose the hill, above the hill rose the barrow, and above
> the barrow rose the figure.

The similar passage in *The Prelude*, VIII, is familiar.
Wordsworth first saw man as a single human figure on a
hilltop.

> Or him have I descried in distant sky,
> A solitary object and sublime,
> Above all height! like an aerial Cross
> As it is stationed on some spiry Rock
> Of the Chartreuse for worship. Thus was man
> Ennobled outwardly before mine eyes.

Once he had sighted man Wordsworth paid to him his due.
Man is "lord and master . . . of all visible natures crown."
He is "more than anything we know, instinct with God-
head."

But the poet, like the reddleman, felt no personal identity with this crowning fact in nature, save as he communed with nature in its entirety. Wordsworth, except
for rare moments of semi-mystical fulfillment, is always
careful to observe the distinction between the objects he

contemplates and himself as thinking subject. There is a gulf between. And man was for him an incident in the scene unfolded on the far side of the gulf.

Wordsworth is almost wholly wanting in social mysticism. In his earlier years of political idealism he had tried to identify himself with other men. But "social man" had proved intractable. That man had been wayward, defiant, and disobedient to the heavenly vision. He had answered the summons of art with insolence. He had revolted not merely against kings, he had revolted against poets. For Wordsworth this last rebellion was the worst. By 1794–95 he had lost interest in man the political animal. As the golden decade dawns we find Wordsworth quite dissociated from humanity, standing alone over against the totality of things. Other men belonged with rocks and stones and trees, as facts in nature. Had his political enthusiasms been vindicated we might have had in Wordsworth that sense of passionate identity with humanity which we find in John Woolman or in Tolstoi. But this idea never matured in his verse.

The want of social mysticism is a defect in Wordsworth. The world of human affairs had been not only too much with him, but too much for him. The shepherd over against him on the sky-line should ideally have been by his side. But, on the other hand, this relegation of man to a place on the far side of the gulf enabled Wordsworth to deal with him poetically. The subject-matter for poems must be malleable. Imagination should be able to bend the chosen theme to its own uses and purposes. Your subject cannot be truculent. An early critic of Wordsworth's verse says that the leech-gatherer means nothing without the lonely moor, and that the two "coalesce in one moving image." The poet's control of man became possible only as he identified man with a natural order which was lending itself generously to re-creation in art. Had Wordsworth kept man — all other men or any single individual — on his side of the gulf he would have been quite unable to make poetic use of him. Wordsworth asked no creative help from other men, and welcomed no shy offers of aid. He demanded only that his human subjects should be passive until he chose to woo them with his imagination. He insisted upon the self-sufficing power of his own solitariness as an artist.

This was nature's excellence, as Wordsworth rediscovered it at the beginning of his first productive period. She did not answer back; or, if she answered him, it was with reassuring echoes and not in tones which truculently defied his gentle invitation to verse. Whether the order of nature is in fact the entity which Wordsworth conceived it to be, endless "goings-on" penetrated by an "eternity of thought" and sustained by that thought, may be an open question. I am not discussing the accuracy of Wordsworth's interpretation of nature. It is not peculiar to himself, being in essence Stoic and meriting whatever sanctions derive from the elder system. Wordsworth may be right about the order of nature; he may be wrong. That is not the point. The immediate point is this: the forms of nature which he knew best offered William Wordsworth workable material for poetry at a time when the human themes to which he had addressed himself for six or seven years had proved to be unprofitable because intractable. And as a poet he had a right to such a subject, for poetry is impossible on any other terms.

How serviceable the Lake District was to him. It was not merely second nature in memory; it was also inherently stimulating and manageable. One cannot conceive of any other two or three hundred square miles of this earth's face better suited to his demand than were his own Cumberland and Westmorland. His prose suggests that he was keenly alive to the peculiar fitness of the scene to his need after he had remanded himself in maturity to nature. In his *Guide through the Lakes in the North of Eng-*

land and in the *Kendal and Windermere Railway* he lingers gratefully over the highly individualized scenes spread before him.

I do not know any tract of country in which, within so narrow a compass, may be found an equal variety in the influences of light and shadow upon the sublime or beautiful features of landscape. . . .

Every valley has its distinct and separate character; in some instances as if they had been formed in studied contrast to each other, and in others with the united pleasing differences and resemblances of a sisterly rivalship. . . .

But to proceed with our survey; — and, first of the MOUNTAINS. Their *forms* are endlessly diversified, sweeping easily or boldly in simple majesty, abrupt and precipitous, or soft and elegant. In magnitude and grandeur they are individually inferior to the most celebrated of those in some other parts of this island; but, in the combinations which they make, towering above each other, or lifting themselves in ridges like the waves of a tumultuous sea, and in the beauty and variety of their surfaces and colours, they are surpassed by none. . . .

I shall now speak of the Lakes of this country. . . . In Switzerland and Scotland, the proportion of diffused water is often too great. . . .

It may now be proper to say a few words respecting the "skiey influences" . . . a country of mists and clouds and storms make him think of the blank sky of Egypt and of the cerulean vacancy of Italy, as an unanimated and even a sad spectacle. . . .

The COTTAGES . . . may rather be said to have grown than to have been erected; to have arisen by an instinct of their own out of the native rock. . . .

These running comments indicate how tractable for his uses Wordsworth found the scene. He is at great pains in one passage to prove that mountains 3,000 feet high are

better subjects for poems than mountains of 14,000 or
15,000 feet. Save for the passage about the descent of the
Simplon Pass Wordsworth's journeys through the Alps
yielded him little first-rate verse. He seems to have found
them too massive to be subjugated by his imagination.
Hence he is careful to vindicate the greater excellence of
the lesser hills which were his horizon-line. Here was a
natural scene, grave to the point of melancholy, which
fitted his mood; a prospect variegated enough to prompt
the associative process of his mind and to provide at every
turn the paradox of dissimilitude in similitude; a scene
of restricted dimensions in each direction so that the imagination was not a "prostrate, overborne pensioner."
Wordsworth was always able to re-create the Lake District
and yet to keep faith with it in so doing. Given his history,
his temperament, and his needs in the hour when he was
remanded to nature, one can only say that Wordsworth
was happy in his home. No other scene stirred him in like
manner; and many scenes left him unmoved, either because they were not part of remembered years of earlier
sensibility or because they were insipid, monotonous, and
unmanageable. Had his early life and his genius been different, he might have done for the fen-country to the north
and east of Cambridge what he did for the Lake District.
Indeed, had he been the child of that shire, Cambridge
itself might have had from him the one poem which she
has lacked, her *Scholar Gipsy*! But then he would not have
been Wordsworth. The espousal of his mind to the Lake
District was an inevitable love affair of his spiritual maturity. Therefore, when discussing Wordsworth's treatment
of nature we should realize fully that he dealt with nature
in particular, rather than nature in general, — nature in a
single aspect lending herself to his need and to his genius.

A recent criticism of Wordsworth's attitude toward
nature takes exception to precisely the element of tracta-
bility which we have been discussing:

The Wordsworthian adoration of Nature has two principal defects. The first . . . is that it is only possible in a country where Nature has been nearly or quite enslaved to man. . . . Europe is so well gardened that it resembles a work of art. . . . Man has recreated Europe in his own image. Its tamed and temperate Nature confirmed Wordsworth in his philosophisings.[1]

The modern char-à-banc has undoubtedly enslaved the Lake District of today, although the place has never been turned to economic account. But it was relatively wild and untamed when William and Dorothy settled in Grasmere. As a playground it was less invaded during all of Wordsworth's lifetime than are the Swiss Alps in our time. We should beware of the anachronism which crowds Wordsworth's lonely vales with our jostling tourists and which imputes our motoring speed to the manner of Wordsworth's leisurely arrival at Dove Cottage. Much of the district, as he first knew it, was inviolate and untenanted. That, however, is not the point. Poetry has never been successful with natural scenes which are vast, rarely visited, and quite uninhabited. You must have lived long with so much of nature as is to become the theme for your poem. Dr. Wilson, of the Scott South Polar party, wrote a few moving lines about the Antarctic Ice Barrier, but they are not great poetry. Wordsworth's tamed themes from nature may be defended on the ground that every poetic subject, to be amenable to the operations of a poet's imagination, must be so well known as to have become second mental nature. If this be enslavement, then all proper subjects for poetry walk in chains.

Mr. Huxley's next indictment of Wordsworth is more serious:

The second is that it [i.e. Wordsworth's adoration of Nature] is only possible for those who are, prepared to falsify their im-

---

1. Aldous Huxley, *Do What You Will* (London: Chatto and Windus, 1929), p. 116, as quoted by Norman Kemp Smith, "Is Divine Existence Credible?" *Proceedings of the British Academy. Volume XVII* (London: Humphrey Milford).

mediate intuitions of Nature. For Nature, even in the temperate zone, is always alien and unknown, and occasionally diabolic. . . . Our direct intuitions of Nature tell us that the world is bottomlessly strange; alien, even when it is kind and beautiful; having innumerable modes of being that are not our modes; always mysteriously not personal, not conscious, not moral; often hostile and sinister; sometimes even unimaginably, because inhumanly, evil. . . . A voyage through the tropics would have cured [Wordsworth] of his too easy and comfortable pantheism. A few months in the jungle would have convinced him that the diversity and utter strangeness of Nature are at least as real and significant as its intellectually discovered unity. Nor would he have felt as certain, in the damp and stifling darkness, among the leeches and the malevolently tangled rattans, of the divinely anglican character of that fundamental unity.

In defense of Wordsworth it should be said that not all persons who have been in the jungle think as badly of it as Mr. Huxley thinks. The arguments which he elaborates have been appreciably deflated in recent years, and many terrors conjured up by a priori theories about the diabolic element in the struggle for existence have proved not as fearful in fact as they were in anticipation. The whole theory that communing with nature is rather like "cuddling up to a Siberian tiger" is being revised before our eyes. The Arctic has been declared friendly, the Himalayas are confidently prophesied as a playground, and explorers in the tropics deal with leeches and rattans as annoyances rather than as visible incarnations of Satanism.

Such considerations apart, it is entirely unjust to indict Wordsworth for failing to solve in advance of its statement the ethical problem raised by the evolutionary theory. What he might have had to say on this matter, had he read Huxley's Romanes Lecture on *Evolution and Ethics*, we cannot tell. He might well have taken service under Kropotkin's banner, continuing to affirm what he had affirmed, the mutual aid which living things give to one another. Had this been his course he would still have been in reputable company. Indeed, Wordsworth might be written down as a forerunner of Kropotkin, for the very term which the latter uses to describe the biological process is found in the former:

Creatures that in communities exist . . .
through dependence upon mutual aid.[1]

But Wordsworth was not primarily concerned with the manner in which leeches or Siberian tigers survive. The nature with which he communed was predominantly the inanimate world: clouds, winds, and sleety rain. His affinities are with astronomy, geology, and the like, rather than with biology. I do not observe even in the modern world, which professes to be gravely perplexed over the moral problem as stated in the terms of natural processes, that the temper has changed substantially since Wordsworth's day in the areas which he habitually cultivated. The natural scientists whom I know best, working in the fields which Wordsworth occupied, are, like the poet, men of cheerful yesterdays and confident tomorrows. They may not follow him to his bolder conclusions, but, on the other hand, they are not oppressed by injustices and inhumanly evil intimations rising like a stench from their subject-matter. They occupy much the position which Wordsworth occupied; nature endures our scrutiny and in the end yields us her secret as knowledge. She is not averse to being wooed by the human mind. It is true that you will not find the Wordsworth temper among those thinkers who are still living on the funeral baked meats of the struggle for existence as it was conceived a generation ago. If this is your only moral diet, you will go unfed at Wordsworth's board. But I venture to think that many affinities with Wordsworth may be marked among persons whose intellectual traffic is with the stars, the elements, and the rocks. There are reputable living astronomers, physicists, ge-

1. *The Excursion*, IV, 440.

ologists, who do not find the poet either incredible or un-congenial. Therefore I protest against exiling or silencing Wordsworth, when he speaks of nature, merely because his verse was not able to reckon with certain vexed ethical issues which arose after his time.

Moreover, when Wordsworth speaks of the "moral" quality which he discerns in nature, that quality is not to be sought in ethical ends which nature proposes to herself. On the contrary, nature is called moral because she lends herself to our thoughts and feelings. This is nature's goodness, that she may be known and loved by us. Possibly we have here an arbitrary definition of morality, but we must allow his words to mean what the poet intended. His brief for nature's morality was based upon her openness to our address. In his sense of the word, therefore, nature has become increasingly moral as in the past century we have come to know her better. The transactions which Charles Darwin had with her were a vindication of her essential goodness. It is doubtful how much more Wordsworth claimed for nature, in the realm of ethics. But he never claimed less, and his theory that there is a moral principle in all things, coercing them into unity, has been defended scientifically, as he vindicated it poetically.

Meanwhile William Wordsworth was never sentimental in the presence of nature. The austerity of his subject was matched by a hardness in his own character. There was a fearless candor in his verse. The natural order as he contemplated it was unfallen and unashamed. "He denuded nature of all her drapery with which humanity had invested her from the dawn of creation, and contemplated her in her nakedness," [1] yet his gaze never profaned her. In that gaze we identify what Sir Walter Raleigh has called "the calm and terrible strength of his best work."

1. *Fraser's Magazine*, VI (1832), 613.

CHAPTER XI

Religion

COLERIDGE said, at the time their friendship began in 1796, that Wordsworth was a "semi-atheist." The connotation of the term is uncertain. He probably meant that Wordsworth was not an orthodox Church of England Christian. Critics, however, have been at great pains to fasten upon Coleridge's remark and to enlarge upon the contrast between the unfettered godlessness of the poet's youth and the perfunctory piety of his later years. The exchange of atheism for Anglicanism is supposed to be one of the aspects of Wordsworth's anti-climax.

I find it hard to subscribe to such an account of Wordsworth's spiritual history. He is one of those men, and they are not uncommon, whose deeper nature contains an unstratified, elemental religiousness, and whose superficial character shows theological strata not derived from the basic substance. Wordsworth, the Anglican with high-church leanings, does not persuade us that either the theory or the practice required by his churchmanship went very deep. On the other hand, his earlier work, so far from being aggressively atheistic, makes constant and uncritical use of conventional religious ideas. God is invoked, the Savior is recognized, the cross is cited, and sentiments of unimpeachable piety are put into the mouths of his characters at precisely the time when he was supposedly an atheist. We do not get the impression that during the 1790's Wordsworth allowed his heroes and heroines to use expressions which would have been insincere had they appeared in a more autobiographical context. The inference is that he imputed to his characters religious conventions which he employed uncritically and as a matter of course, because they were second nature to him.

We may suppose that during his school and university days Wordsworth had been exposed to conventional Christianity and that its vocabulary formed part of his mental patrimony. The whole impression given us of the man from his twentieth to his thirtieth year is that of one who had inherited the doctrines and symbols of Christianity, whose deeper nature remained untouched by them, and who used them in his work as occasion arose without stopping to ask whether they were true or how far he believed them. Had Wordsworth been an aggressive atheist, after Shelley's pattern, we should have had in the earlier work, if not a frontal attack on orthodoxy, at least a studied avoidance of any reference to traditional religion.

The later years of his life give much the same suggestion. Wordsworth became, in theory even more fully than in practice, an Anglican. But his Anglicanism did not require conscious conversion or change in his manner of life. He resumed, once he was settled at Grasmere, the church routine that had been familiar to him in his youth. His enthusiasm for the Church of England is quite intelligible. The church, more effectually perhaps than the state, was the custodian of tradition, the vindicator of the social contract in history, as Burke had defined it. "The noble Living and the noble Dead" were more real in church than elsewhere. Wordsworth said in so many words that he regarded the Church of England as the strongest buttress of the English Constitution, and therefore as necessary to the life of the nation. He had none of that devotion to the church as an end in itself which carried Newman over to Rome, and which made Keble a saint within Anglican orders. The church was to him a means to ends, which, if not political, were cultural rather than theological.

At the time of his graduation from Cambridge he expected, for the want of a better option, to take orders. To do so was a matter of course rather than of conviction. Dorothy writing in 1790 says, "When he will go into Orders I do not know. . . . He must when he is three-and-twenty, either go into Orders or take pupils." The trip abroad, for the sake of perfecting his French, seems to suggest that by the fall of 1791 Wordsworth's mind leaned in the latter direction. On May 17, 1792, he writes to William Mathews from Blois, "It is at present my intention to take orders in the approaching winter or spring. . . . Had it been in my power I should certainly have wished to defer the moment." Apparently the affair with Annette had made Wordsworth question his fitness for ordination.

After his settlement at Grasmere, his marriage, and the coming of the children, we find Wordsworth, with Dorothy and Mary, back at church. They went, we are told in the journals and letters, mainly for the sake of the children. But they "took turns." There was not much inducement to church-going in the Grasmere of 1800. The rector had been an imbecile for years, and the curate who served in his stead was a drunkard. Things subsequently improved, but Wordsworth in the pews was seldom faced by a kindred spirit in the pulpit:

Miss Hutchinson and I were at church yesterday. We were pleased with the singing; and I have often heard a far worse parson — I mean as to reading. His sermon was, to be sure, as village sermons often are, very injudicious; a most knowing discourse about the Gnostics, and other hard names of those who were *h*adversaries to Christianity and *h*enemies of the Gospel. . . . I don't know that I ever heard in a country pulpit a sermon that had any special bearing on the condition of the majority of the audience.[1]

---

1. W. W. to Sir George Beaumont, November 10, 1806.

As the children grew up, the dutiful habit of church-going seems to have been relaxed. There is an amusing description of Wordsworth in later life vehemently defending in one breath the Church of England, and then admitting in the next breath that he could not remember when he had last been to church! The paradox tells volumes about his Anglicanism.

As for his high-church propensities, though unlikely in an independent north-country Englishman, they are intelligible. Crabb Robinson says that Wordsworth moved in this direction because high-churchmen had a greater reverence for antiquity than the evangelicals. And Dean Inge has pointed out that the drift of ideas which issued in the Oxford Movement was determined by the doctrine of the Incarnation rather than of the Atonement. The latter doctrine was stressed by the evangelicals, and the former was much more consonant with Wordsworth's theory of the "Presence."

The poet himself made increasingly orthodox protestations as the years went on, though he disclaimed any accurate knowledge of theological issues and refrained from being a religious poet after the manner of Montgomery. He insisted upon the "distinction between religion in poetry and versified religion," and refused to venture in the latter field. His *Ecclesiastical Sonnets* contains fine lines, and was his contribution to the cause of tradition; but it is conventional as history and unimportant as theology. Biblical scholars often refer students to Browning's *Death in the Desert* for a penetrating insight into the conditions which yielded us the Fourth Gospel. I have never known a church historian make the slightest use of Wordsworth's sonnets on Anglicanism, and few of us have ever read them twice or gained from them any deeper understanding of the thousand years of English Christianity.

When I think of Wordsworth the Anglican, I see him meandering about the churchyard, studying the epitaphs

and reluctant to heed the summons of the church bell.
Once in church he has little interest in sacraments and
sermons. His eyes are wandering around the walls, and his
mind is prophetically busy with the inscription in memory
of 𝖘𝖎𝖗 𝕬𝖑𝖋𝖗𝖊𝖉 𝕴𝖗𝖙𝖍𝖎𝖓𝖌 which he proposes to read at leisure
after the benediction has been pronounced. Wordsworth
would have made an admirable verger and sexton, but an
indifferent priest. He loved the Church of England, not
because it provided sermons and sacraments, but because
it kept in its perpetual care the memory of the successive
generations of his fellow-countrymen. Within its acre tradition was powerfully felt and the continuity of the English
nation guaranteed. Realizing how much of the talk of *The
Excursion* took place in the graveyard outside the church
among the mountains and how little inside its four walls,
he tells us that he was at pains to order it so, that the conversation might have as its background permanent and
enduring forms of nature, the elder sisters of all human
institutions. The attempt to discover Wordsworth's religion within the Thirty-nine Articles can only end in a caricature of that religion. If we wish the best Anglican poetry
of the first half of the last century we should close our
Wordsworth and open our Keble. As versified religion the
Ecclesiastical Sonnets is no match for *The Christian Year*.

Nor can I see anything to be gained from the attempt to
get Wordsworth transplanted into some church other than
the one to which he professed loyalty. The Quakers have
claimed him as their own. The Unitarians have found him
congenial. The disciples of Spinoza have hailed him as a
prophet, second in authority only to their master. Pantheists have made him their high priest. For nearly a century
now his bones have been picked by quarreling sects, each
of which claims the right to keep the shrine where he is to
be theologically entombed and honored. But Wordsworth as a religious genius cannot be monopolized by any
denomination.

A prior problem is more pertinent. Was Wordsworth ever a Christian, even on the most generous construction of the word? *The Eclectic Review* thought not, and made Montgomery its head inquisitor to challenge his heresies, its chief mourner to lament his defects. We concede Wordsworth his prose professions of orthodoxy during the later years. But what of the poetry? Does it fall inside any scheme of things which can be called Christian? Charles Lamb was mildly exercised over the matter. "Is the Poet of the 'Excursion' a Christian? Or is it the Pedlar and the Priest that are?" Granted, as Montgomery said, that "the true cross does not bulk large among Wordsworth's trees," and that "redemption in the blood" is not a major Wordsworthian idea, what of his doctrine of God? This threshing-floor has been blown clean. It has been pointed out that in the earliest poems Wordsworth seems to have believed in God-the-Creator, that he then passed on to a pantheistic faith which served him through his greatest years, that subsequently he took pains to insist upon a distinction between God and nature, and that finally he stressed the indwelling God rather than God the external creator and governor. That Wordsworth believed in God is beyond contradiction. That he never was able to define in so many words what he meant by the term, and that his emphases changed with the successive periods of his life seems clear. In these respects he was not unlike any other thoughtful man and is under no special condemnation. You may find in Wordsworth passages in defense of your own idea of God, whatever it may be, or in defense of some principle of impersonality which hardly deserves the name of God. The poems are a mine yielding more than one kind of theological ore. I see no possibility of harmonizing all their religious ideas, and much difficulty in tracing the shifting emphasis with the passage of the years. You may call Wordsworth a Christian poet with much propriety; you may with equal propriety construe him as non-Chris-

tian. The evidence is so considerable and ambiguous that
no single conclusion is inevitable.

I do not think that these details matter. As a reader of
Wordsworth I am uninterested in the attempt to identify
the precise measure of Christianity, of theism or of pantheism, in his verse. Wordsworth seems to me to be religious
at that deeper, undifferentiated level where distinctions
hardly obtain. He manifests the elemental genius of all
religions and of any religion. There is only one of our
specialized types of religion of which he became eventually
incapable, the religion of humanism, — unless humanism
be construed as communion with an ideal race to the entire
neglect of actual men. Wordsworth had, until the end of
the Godwin period, the possibility of becoming one of the
great spokesmen for humanism, but with his disillusionment as to "social man" his religion of humanity died
slowly away. He continued to profess faith in some abstract communion of political saints, but he had little
spiritual companionship with living men. His religion, as
we have it in his mature work, is the cosmic faith, man's
spiritual traffic with an infinite universe. The outward and
visible symbols of infinity he found in the forms of nature.
He did not think it beneath his dignity to draw the boldest
inferences from the least occasions:

> The commerce between Man and his Maker cannot be carried
> on but by a process where much is represented in little, and the
> Infinite Being accommodates himself to a finite capacity.

Wordsworth speaks here as an artist, for it is the custom
of art to seek its universals in concrete facts, even in humble and familiar facts. But saints also have often found
much in little, and Wordsworth's poetry has, in its tempers,
many affinities with the classics of devotional literature.

Meanwhile, there are two or three constant ideas in
Wordsworth which constitute him, in the generic sense of
the word, a religious poet, and which may be identified in

certain words used so often that they were little short of mannerisms. Once our attention has been called to them, their frequency is almost annoying. The first group of these words serve the idea of solitude. Professor Whitehead has said,

> The great religious conceptions which haunt the imagination of civilized mankind are scenes of solitariness; Prometheus chained to his rock, Mahomet brooding in the desert, the meditations of the Buddha, the solitary man on his Cross. Religion is what the individual does with his solitariness . . . and if you are never solitary you are never religious.

Whitehead's judgment parts company with all accounts of religion as a survival of the folkways of primitive man. It presupposes self-conscious individuality, and the civilized man to whom it applies emerged from the herd four or five centuries before our era. We meet him in both the Greek and the Hebrew traditions. Since his emergence it has been unnecessary to prove to him his loneliness, and whatever its primitive origin or its ultimate destiny as a social fact, modern religion is always in some measure "the flight of the alone to the Alone."

There are no words more characteristic of Wordsworth than those which ring changes on the idea of solitude.[1] And there is no English poet of whom it can be said with anything like equal truth that his scenes of solitariness haunt our imagination. He sings a solitary song, and the plaintive spirit of lonely places is heard in his verse. The setting of all his best work is that most likely to breed "great religious conceptions."

Wordsworth takes it for granted that we shall understand him. He appeals to a universal human experience. Nevertheless in this, as in so many kindred matters, his vocabulary has a technical connotation which we must

---

1. Cf. A. C. Bradley, *Oxford Lectures on Poetry* (London: Macmillan Company, 1909), pp. 141–143.

identify if we are to get his shades of meaning. The essence
of solitariness is with him an immunity to sense experiences. Either we have never had strong sensations, or
having had them have outgrown them. In solitariness the
operations of eye and ear are "almost suspended." The
pensive traveler "treads the lonesome path with unobserv-
ing eye"; the blind boy grows up "in loneliness of soul"
because he has been denied sight of the world without.

Speaking of himself, Wordsworth says that after his first
period of sensibility was over,

> I had been trained up to stand unpropp'd,
> And independent musings pleased me so
> That spells seemed on me when I was alone,
> Yet could I only cleave to solitude
> In lonesome places.

Here again is the curious description of the outer order as
the prop of our affections. Loneliness is an unpropped
state of life, a want of the buttresses which nature lays
against the surface of the senses.

In this sensationless state of being we are preoccupied
with our thoughts. An inner intentness, expectancy, and
invention ensue. Finally imagination, the mind's creative energy, asserts itself. Unlike fancy, or even trains
of imagery, imagination requires an actual fact for its
subject-matter, and the creative soul turns again to the
natural world from which it has been temporarily withdrawn. Imagination thus oriented finds in nature, or imputes to it, an energy kindred to itself. The lonely poet's
vigilant spirit is mated with the souls of lonely places, with
"the solitary sheep, the solitary tree, the solitary tarn."
It is as though the creative power in nature were thought
of as being fully self-conscious only when it is incarnate in
single objects.

When he was in the imaginative vein, the solitary objects in nature seemed to Wordsworth to advance to meet
him. Thus in the familiar and mysterious passage which

describes the huge peak striding across the lake in the dusk
toward his motionless boat:

> in my thoughts
> There was a darkness, call it solitude,
> Or blank desertion, no familiar shapes
> Of hourly objects, images of trees,
> Or sea or sky, no colours of green fields;
> But huge and mighty Forms that do not live
> Like living men mov'd slowly through the mind.

Desertion is here the synonym for solitude. The imagination moves about in worlds that cannot be realized by the
senses. Sensation has been dismissed in "fallings from us,
vanishings," and imagination as the creative principle in
both the poet and the natural scene comes alive. The
senses tell you nothing about the souls of solitary places;
only imagination can discern that soul, working confeder-
ately in both man and nature.

In inviting such an experience at any time after his
healthful remand to nature, Wordsworth laid himself open
to a recurrence of the malady of a too great subjectivity
from which he had suffered during his years of despondency. The play of fancy had been costly to him and must
always have remained dangerous. How far, in the elaboration of his idea of solitude in *The Prelude*, Wordsworth is
remembering the past, and how far he is describing the
esthetic regimen of his psychology, almost ritual in its
deliberateness, we cannot say. As for the Solitary of *The
Excursion*, he was not a man on whom the poet looked back
with pleasure or approval. In the figure he has painted a
picture of the sorry consequences of solitude uncorrected.
Elsewhere Wordsworth admits in so many words that he
had been

> taught to feel, perhaps too much,
> The self-sufficing power of solitude.

The last line ought never to be torn from its context. It is
a warning to be heeded, not a maxim to be followed.

But solitariness was, nevertheless, a necessary condition for Wordsworth's art. It was part of the price he paid and of the risk he ran in being a poet. He discusses the conditions for poetry as though he were dealing with high-tension wires, required for his task yet dangerous to handle, or were taking some powerful stimulant, salutary within limits but deadly in excess.

In his conception and conduct of the regimen of solitude Wordsworth has been matched by many other mystics. A preliminary detachment from the too insistent world of sense, an introversion and deliberate recollection are necessary preliminaries for creative insights. The lonely Wordsworth belongs to a well-recognized and reputable society of persons who "all come from the same country and speak the same language." His technique for the making of poems should be compared with the stages of the mystic's *scala perfectionis*.

Wordsworth's confidence in the commerce of his creative spirit with a kindred energy in the souls of lonely places suggests a second verbal convention in his verse, which puts him still more certainly within the circle of the religious idea — his habit of using paired, antithetical words. A religious vocabulary makes constant use of the paradox, not as a verbal trick, but as witness to ultimate contrasts which religion states and then attempts to reconcile. Religion is not peculiar in this respect. The great words of the language always travel in pairs, — day and night, winter and summer, heat and cold, man and woman, work and rest, war and peace. If our speech contents itself with words which can stand alone, requiring no complement, we may be reasonably certain that it is not concerned with elemental facts or universal experiences. However this may be in other areas of life, it is certainly true in religion. "Look upon all the works of God and there are two and two, one against the other." Secularism may work with words one of a kind, but religion requires an antithesis and the tension resulting from it. Indeed the energy of religion is part of that tension. Thus, God and man, the infinite and the finite, the immortal and the mortal, heaven and hell, eternity and time, life and death, good and evil, sin and repentance, guilt and forgiveness. The essence of all heresy is the attempt to make one of the partners in an antinomy do duty for both, and any such word standing alone is the symptom of a religion which is dying of over-simplification.

Religion's use of the paradox may be verified by reference to any accredited book of devotion, — St. Augustine's *Confessions*, Pascal's *Pensées*, the *Book of Common Prayer*. Once your attention has been called to the convention you are amazed to find how constant it is. Religion is speaking naturally when it prays with the Breton fisherman, "O God, thy sea is so great and my boat is so small"; when it cries out with Augustine, "Our hearts are restless until they find rest in thee."

Now Wordsworth's vocabulary is freighted with paired words, one against the other. He stressed the importance, for art, of "the principle of similitude in dissimilitude," and he invoked the principle to explain the pleasure which we get from poetry. A skilful use of meter gives us the surprise of change together with the reassurance had from constancy. But Wordsworth did not limit the application of the principle to the practice of art as it varies the "repeat" of its pattern. He went on to say that "upon the accuracy with which similitude in dissimilitude and dissimilitude in similitude are perceived" our moral feelings depend. He uses the word "moral" here as elsewhere to suggest, not ethics, but that correspondence between man and his world which is the essence of his poetic experience, which is indeed his religion.

As the words "lonely," "solitary," "loneliness," "solitude" are characteristic of Wordsworth, so also are paired words, two and two, one against the other. They may be had for the asking on almost any page of his work. Very often they concern contrasts on the face of nature: "sunshine and shower," "sky and earth," "east and west," "day and night." Likewise, of the varying moods and contents of human experience: "ill or good," "malice and true love," "to gladden or to grieve," "hurts and heals," "fear and trembling hope," "alive to all things and forgetting all." We might suspect that this verbal convention had its origins in a mental laziness which finds it easier to write two words where one will do, were it not that the usage is rooted in Wordsworth's whole theory of poetry.

Solitariness is a state which cries out for complement. It is the condition in which we realize vividly the half a life we live when we are restricted to ourselves. In practice Wordsworth used loneliness as a device for discovering his kinship with the natural world. Whether or not such communion is the maturest form of religion, whether it meets the requirements of the ethical idea, whether it can continue to satisfy us, — these questions are beside the mark. For better or for worse Wordsworth's religion was a commerce with some imaginative principle in things at once other and greater than himself, unlike him and yet like him.

Wordsworth's theology elaborated to explain his religion is to be found in his prefaces, where he defines the vocation of the poet. On any generous count the poet, as Wordsworth conceives him, is a man who by virtue of his experience falls within the circle of the religious idea. Thus he is

a man pleased with his own passions and volitions . . . delighting to contemplate similar passions and volitions as manifested in the goings-on of the Universe.

He considers man and the objects that surround him as acting and reacting upon each other, so as to produce an infinite complexity of pain and pleasure.

[The poet has] a deep impression of certain inherent and indestructible qualities of the human mind, and likewise of certain
powers in the great and permanent objects that act upon it,
which are equally inherent and indestructible.

He considers man and nature as essentially adapted to each
other, and the mind of man as naturally the mirror of the fairest
and most interesting properties of nature.

The same idea appears in Wordsworth's verse in one of
his most characteristic passages:

> My voice proclaims
> How exquisitely the individual mind
> . . . to the external world
> Is fitted: — and how exquisitely, too —
> This theme but little heard among men —
> The external world is fitted to the mind.

Given this faith, the poet faced his world expecting to be
mated by it:

> Whate'er
> I saw, or heard, or felt, was but a stream
> That flow'd into a kindred stream.

Once his imagination had found its proper subject in the
natural scene, Wordsworth's mind worked in alliance with
the world which it beheld. It is the suggestion of one
"*active* Principle . . . in all things, in all natures," which
gives to his descriptions of man and the outer world the
hint of pantheism with which he is so often charged.

It is wholly useless to split hairs. Was Wordsworth a
pantheist or a theist? There are passages which lend themselves to a pantheistic reading, perhaps require it. The
familiar lines from *Tintern Abbey* are open to this construction:

> A motion and a spirit, that impels
> All thinking things, all objects of all thought.

Perhaps the most unequivocal statement of the idea is that in *The Excursion*, Book IX, which attempts a further definition of the "motion and spirit,"

> An *active* Principle . . .
>   subsists
> In all things, in all natures. . . .
> Spirit that knows no insulated spot,
> No chasm, no solitude; from link to link
> It circulates, the Soul of all the worlds.

If the passage stood alone as Wordsworth's only utterance on these matters, it might throw him into the general area of thought connoted by the term "pantheism." But for the pantheist there is no problem of evil, and Wordsworth's poetry is much too burdened with the heavy weight and the unintelligibility of that problem to leave him long at ease among pantheists or to allow us to classify him as of this society. Many of his lines to the contrary, his preoccupation with the darker side of human experience, his vision of

> the train
> Where beasts and men together o'er the plain
> Move on — a mighty caravan of pain,

as well as his struggle to transmute life's agonizing sorrows put him ultimately beyond the pale of that "mild pantheism" to which a superficial reading of his works has so often assigned him.

Meanwhile, if we take the poet at his word and allow him his uninsulated active principle circling through all things, it is still true that such a "circulation" is made possible only by positive and negative poles. For Wordsworth these poles existed, as his solitary self and the Wisdom and Spirit of the Universe. There was a common principle at work in both, but the distinction between his own mind and the imaginative power in nature was never obliterated. He is careful

                              to keep
            In wholesome separation the two natures,
            The one that feels, the other that observes.

The religious quality which we sense in Wordsworth's
verse, but find it hard to identify, thus resolves itself into a
succession of paradoxes which he uses to describe himself
when employed with works of the imagination. He is subservient to external things, yet an auxiliar light comes from
his mind which gives new splendor to the setting sun. He
is at once "a sensitive being, a creative soul." He is, in the
presence of the outer world, "creator and receiver both."

In the high transaction of poetry there is

            A balance, an ennobling interchange
            Of action from within and from without;
            The excellence, pure spirit, and best power
            Both of the object seen, and eye that sees.

The creative energy which nature manifests is

                        a genuine Counterpart
            And Brother of the glorious faculty
            Which higher minds bear with them as their own.
            That is the very spirit in which they deal
            With all the objects of the universe;
            They from their native selves can send abroad
            Like transformations, for themselves create
            A like existence.

The traffic of imagination with the world furnishes "endless occupation for the Soul" and with Wordsworth suf-
ficed for a religion.

So long as the antithesis was felt and recorded, Wordsworth remained outside the bounds of pantheism, which
is a matter of a single idea and a single mood. With
Wordsworth the poetic act was complex and compound.
He does not attempt to identify the initiative in the transaction. In theory he seems to imply that the priority belongs to nature and to that "eternity of thought" which

he discerned in her.   In practice, however, he assumes, —
what every religious man knows, — that there is no finding
without a seeking.   Thus at one moment he pays his due to
nature and

> from her receives
> That energy by which he seeks the truth.

But at another he is persuaded that

> thou must give,
> Else never canst receive.

The unresolved contradiction is witness to the genuineness
of Wordsworth's experience. If he had stopped in his
verse-making, to discuss the meaning of the paradox, inspiration would have deserted him. He records the experience as he knew it, and the record reveals precisely that
strange duality which we find in all deeply religious utterances.

It is in this elemental commerce of his imagination with
a kindred creative power in nature that Wordsworth's religion is to be found. Off this solid ground we get into
quicksands of doctrinal theology and ecclesiasticism in
which he had no interest, where he was by his own confession incompetent, and which to do him justice he did
his best to avoid. Now and then undiscriminating criticism forced him to try to render first aid to troubled or
offended readers, but he was never successful in his attempts. Wordsworth the poet of the golden decade is certainly not a semi-atheist or an irreligious man, but quite
as certainly he is not an orthodox Christian. The attempt
to prove him such transfers the issue to an area where he
gives us little source-material and leaves us to our own
devices. He told us how he wrote poems, and his experience as a creative artist was essentially the religious experience. We had best let the matter rest there and not
thrust and parry over his disputed soul, using particular

lines wrested from their context in the hope of proving a sectarian case.

Wordsworth's religion was essentially a cosmic experience. I suspect that the present revival of interest in his work is due in part to a spreading conviction that if the universe in its entirety is declared out of bounds for the purposes of religion, religion itself is under sentence of death. I happen to belong to the company of those who believe that

> Our destiny, our nature, and our home
> Is with infinitude, and only there.

For all such Wordsworth's poetry is an intimation of that infinitude, and his poetic interpretation of nature, while not wanting in ethical difficulties, is an insight to be treasured. No other poet in our tradition has spoken of infinity with just his accent or with such authority. The more fully we understand his experience the more willingly we concede his authority.

CHAPTER XII

Ethics

WHEN Frederic Maitland wrote his *Life and Letters of Leslie Stephen* he devoted one chapter to the essay on "Wordsworth's Ethics." [1] Stephen's first wife, Harriet Thackeray, had died in November, 1875, and the Wordsworth essay appeared in *The Cornhill* for August, 1876. He later called it "a lay sermon on the unselfish use of sorrow."

Leslie Stephen says of Wordsworth that "other poetry becomes trifling when we are making our inevitable passage through the Valley of the Shadow of Death: Wordsworth's alone retains its power." Stephen's mind was hard, but his heart was inordinately tender. His study of Wordsworth was prompted by an almost feminine intuition. He was the first to realize how profound Wordsworth's despondency had been, and to take the poet at his own word regarding the correction of despondency. If the affair with Annette had scarred Wordsworth, Stephen's sorrow gave him an insight born of sympathy. On the other hand, if Wordsworth's despondency was a matter of the mind rather than of the heart, Stephen was well calculated to understand the poet. He was honest to a fault and austere in his mental processes. He wished no help, in his sorrow, from those "weak comforters who try to cover up the terrible reality under a veil of well meant fiction. I would rather face the inevitable with open eyes."

1. Stephen's essay may be found in any edition of his *Hours in a Library*.

By 1876 the tedious controversy over Wordsworth's choice of subjects and his poetic diction had worn itself out. For better or for worse he had made his case. There remained, however, the question of his philosophy and its undue intrusion into his verse. Stephen believed that beneath every poetry there lies a philosophy; that great poetry is philosophy. He held that poetry aims to unify our life by ending the divorce between reason and experience. He saw clearly that this had been Wordsworth's purpose, and in his private need he turned to the poet for help.

Wordsworth is the only poet who will bear reading in times of distress. Other poets mock us by an impossible optimism, or merely reflect the feelings which, however we may play with them in times of cheerfulness, have now become an intolerable burden. Wordsworth suggests the single topic which, so far at least as this world is concerned, can really be called consolatory. . . .
All moral teaching, I have sometimes fancied, might be summed up in the one formula, "Waste not." . . . The waste of sorrow is one of the most lamentable forms of waste. Sorrow too often tends to produce bitterness or effeminacy of character. But it may, if rightly used, serve only to detach us from the lower motives, and give sanctity to the higher. That is what Wordsworth sees with unequalled clearness.

If Arnold is right in quoting as Wordsworth's most poetic line the words from *Michael*, "And never lifted up a single stone," Stephen is right in citing as the poet's most philosophic line, "An agonizing sorrow to transmute." The idea there invoked is the substance of Wordsworth's ethics. The poet tells us that the essence of sorrow is not a hurt heart; it is frustrated thought.

> Man is of dust: ethereal hopes are his,
> Which, when they should sustain themselves aloft,
> Want due consistence; like a pillar of smoke,
> That with majestic energy from the earth

Rises; but, having reached the thinner air,
Melts, and dissolves, and is no longer seen.
From this infirmity of mortal kind
Sorrow proceeds, which else were not.

Wordsworth never achieved entire immunity to the malady of absolute idealism. To the end there were times when he went to the facts reluctantly, as a man might lay himself upon a rack for torture. He was always tempted to take refuge in what he had hoped to be and was not, — the citizen of an achieved Utopia:

Whosoe'er in youth
Has, through ambition of his soul, given way
To such desires, and grasped at such delight,
Shall feel congenial stirrings late and long,
In spite of all the weakness that life brings,
Its cares and sorrows; he, though taught to own
The tranquillizing power of time, shall wake,
Wake sometimes to a noble restlessness —
Loving the sports which once he gloried in.

Since such early hopes are seldom fulfilled in fact, the idealist feels the seduction of the contemplative life. He sighs

For independent happiness; craving peace,
The central feeling of all happiness,
Not as a refuge from distress or pain,
A breathing-time, vacation, or a truce,
But for its absolute self; a life of peace,
Stability without regret or fear;
That hath been, is, and shall be evermore.

Wordsworth was prevented from taking shelter in the hermit temper by some strain in him which we may describe as rigorous honesty or Anglo-Saxon common sense. Coleridge found in his friend "something corporeal, a matter-of-factness, a clinging to the palpable." The term does not matter; the quality of mind is patent in the poems. The only peace which the poet's nature allowed him was a

central peace subsisting at the heart
Of endless agitation.

This metaphor sustains longer lines to the same intent:

> The wise
> Have still the keeping of their proper peace;
> Are guardians of their own tranquillity.
> They act, or they recede, observe, and feel;
> 'Knowing the heart of man is set to be
> The centre of this world, about the which
> Those revolutions of disturbances
> Still roll; where all the aspects of misery
> Predominate; whose strong effects are such
> As he must bear, being powerless to redress;
> *And that unless above himself he can*
> *Erect himself, how poor a thing is man!*'

We have here Wordsworth's account of his inner history, put into ordered verse some fifteen or twenty years after his strong disease had yielded to treatment. We are nearer the facts, by a decade, in the first book of *The Prelude*:

> The mind of Man is fram'd even like the breath
> And harmony of music. There is a dark
> Invisible workmanship that reconciles
> Discordant elements, and makes them move
> In one society. Ah me! that all
> The terrors, all the early miseries
> Regrets, vexations, lassitudes, that all
> The thoughts and feelings which have been infus'd
> Into my mind, should ever have made up
> The calm existence that is mine when I
> Am worthy of myself!

The poet does not tell us how the reconciliation is effected, he is content to record the fact. Wordsworth has no monopoly of the idea; we have all verified it in our own experience. If it is not at some later time a pleasure to look back on troubles through which we have passed, at least most troubles lose in retrospect their initial sting and become an intelligible part of life in its entirety. They do not seem irrational or wholly out of part; indeed we more often than otherwise conclude, with Wordsworth, that they have borne a needful part in the making of our maturity.

Wordsworth went on to draw theological inferences from his history, and posited

a Being
Of infinite benevolence and power;
Whose everlasting purposes embrace
All accidents, converting them to good.

If there is any constant idea in Wordsworth's verse which warrants his inclusion within the formal circle inscribed by the Christian idea, it is the confidence that all things may be made to work together for good. His solution of the problem of evil is that of Saint Paul, and his theory about the correction of despondency has striking affinities with the Christian doctrine of atonement. If one is zealous to number Wordsworth among the Christians, he had best rest his case upon the poet's ethics rather than upon his theology. For the Christian religion has always professed to deal with evil as Wordsworth dealt with sorrow, proposing a strange inner alchemy by which it may be transmuted into good.

On the other hand, Wordsworth did not require a theology as the premise for his ethics. His ethics were purely empirical; he observed that the transmutation took place, and as he began to be healed of his distress he recorded his cure. He believed so profoundly in man's power to turn sorrow into joy that he was willing to make of the principle a categorical imperative. We are to meet the darker side of life with the advance intention of reversing the shield. Such considerations may or may not be a proper theme for poetry. They are far removed from spades and sparrows' eggs. It is, moreover, difficult if not impossible to find concrete images for the theory, though it may be suggested in the histories of simple people.

Matthew Arnold was not without grounds for his dislike of Wordsworthianism. But Matthew Arnold and his kind are under bond to explain why Dante and Milton are to be allowed a philosophy or a theology controlling their

verse, while Wordsworth is denied the right. If Adam's
disobedience is a fit theme for poetry, why not William
Wordsworth's despondency? The full majesty of Wordsworth's mind is exhibited only at such levels, even though
he was not as competent as were Dante and Milton to
stage a large action poetically.

Wordsworth's success with humble and rustic themes
leads us to disparage his philosophical poetry. But his
ethics — and by inference his theology — are not absent
from a poem like *Michael*, though they are so skilfully
clothed in simplicity that we do not at once identify the
determining idea. Hence Wordsworth's more reflective
verse often seems less successful than it is.

> Thou hast great allies;
> Thy friends are exultations, agonies,
> And love, and man's unconquerable mind.

This is Wordsworthianism. Of its kind it is powerful
poetry, and we should not allow the peculiar distinction of
the *Lyrical Ballads* to blind us to its excellence. I do not
see how such lines are to be deleted from our Wordsworth,
if we are to be in any way fair to the poet. Nor can I see
that we need go out of our way to avoid them lest we de-
clare ourselves wanting a proper appreciation of poetry in
professing a feeling for them. English verse has always
dared to attempt large ideas.

Moreover we should not allow the discussion of Wordsworthianism to move the issue over on to purely hypo-
thetical grounds. Much of Wordsworth's poetry deals
with religious and ethical subjects. To exclude the poems
written around these interests is to mangle your Wordsworth beyond recognition. It is true that the philosophy
is most effectively communicated when it is suggested
rather than when it is described or defined. But even when
images are used there is a reality behind the appearance.
Margaret and Michael are intimations of a truth which in

the person of the Wanderer is stated more abstractly. In want of the general truth the concrete symbol has no meaning.

Leslie Stephen would reduce all ethical maxims to a single imperative, "Waste not." He intended the words to apply to Wordsworth, and his intention was warranted. Wordsworth hated to lose anything and saved zealously. The trait is most apparent in money matters. Yet his carefulness was not confined to investments. In the poet's meticulous remembrance of his early life there was a kind of moral fanaticism. His psychology had given him full right to look for subjects there; he made it a duty as well, with the result that incidents of ephemeral interest were proposed for literary immortality. Not all the past "spots of time" on which he fastened had the quality of eternal life. Given his psychology and his ethics, however, Wordsworth erred on the right side. The fragments of his experience were all gathered up, and nothing of poetic worth was lost.

As to the waste of sorrow — in Wordsworth's case a mental distress — his verse does not make it clear how the transmutation into joy was achieved. The want of satisfactory analysis is an indication that the experience was real. Had Wordsworth been inventing he would have been more explicit. It is only life itself that is thus inarticulate. Time seems to have been the chief alchemist and to have worked in secret.

By the beginning of the golden decade Wordsworth was prepared to affirm that

> neither evil tongues,
> Rash judgments, nor the sneers of selfish men,
> Nor greetings where no kindness is, nor all
> The dreary intercourse of daily life,
> Shall e'er prevail against us, or disturb
> Our cheerful faith, that all which we behold
> Is full of blessings.

The affirmation remains thereafter the first article of the Wordsworth creed. Yet I confess to a curious feeling of insecurity in presence of the creed. I do not question Wordsworth's sincerity. He was not lying to himself in an endeavor to make a worse appear a better world. As a poet he was persuaded of an excess of pleasure over pain in any given human experience. Hartley had guaranteed such a margin. Wordsworth drew from his esthetics an ethical inference, and was prepared to say that life in its entirety holds more good than evil.

But he seems to have been in much the position which Browning described later: he stood firm upon the serpent just because he felt it writhe; he showed us faith to prove that doubt exists. Whatever we may make of Wordsworth's ethics we should not do them the injustice of dismissing them as the utterance of an inexpert optimist. His bravest pleas in behalf of goodness were made before a back-drop dark with suffering, his own and that of other men. It is true of Wordsworth's ethics, as of those religions which William James commends, that a profound initial pessimism is required to give the ultimate optimism its meaning. Wordsworth, once he was set upon his poetic way, was a man of "confident to-morrows," but he was never self-deceived about evil. In all his greatest verse we hear "the still sad music of humanity"; we brood over "sorrows barricadoed evermore within the walls of cities," we journey with "a mighty caravan of pain."

We sense in Wordsworth's ethics a vigilance as well as a serenity. His ethics were not merely a retrospective appraisal of past life, they were also a plan of action addressed to the rush of oncoming experience, a manner of the mind which could be relied upon to turn the spear point of all that is meant by evil. Hence the suggestion of an action still on, rather than of a battle won.

If any proof is needed of a hint of insecurity in Wordsworth's moralizings we have it in a sentence or two from a letter of Quillinan's to Crabb Robinson (October, 1849):

> You will find your old and faithful friend the poet pretty much as he was on y{superscript}r last visit. The same social cheerfulness — company cheerfulness — the same fixed despondency (uncorrected). I esteem him for both: I love him best for the latter.

Edward Quillinan had come late into the Wordsworth circle. He settled at Rydal in 1822. It was nearly twenty years before the poet would consent to Dora's marrying him. Quillinan was a widower with children, an Irishman, and a Roman Catholic. He was, therefore, a most unlikely son-in-law for William Wordsworth. Since the poet kept him at arm's length for years, Quillinan never became an idolater, and of the immediate circle of family and friends he remained the most detached. His judgments of Wordsworth have an insight given by dispassionateness. Hence the significance of Quillinan's words, "the same despondency (uncorrected)." [1] They confirm the impression given by many of the later poems. Wordsworth's innate melancholy remained to the end, and if we dig deep enough we always find it beneath the more studied cheerfulness.

Let it be said at once that ethically Wordsworth rises to a level far higher than that occupied by either the professional pessimist or the professional optimist. At one extreme the professional optimist wins his moral victories too easily. At the other extreme the professional pessimist relishes his sorrows, and has no honest wish to be relieved of them. At both extremes there is sentimentalism. Whatever his other faults, Wordsworth is, where good and evil are concerned, guiltless of sentimentality. He was much too matter-of-fact to deny the reality of evil, and much too

---

1. Cf. also a letter of Charles Lamb to Wordsworth, 1815, on *Yarrow Visited*: "The poem, on the whole, seems condemned to leave behind it, a melancholy of imperfect satisfaction, as if you had wronged the feeling with which, in what preceded it, you had resolved never to visit it."

resolute to allow himself the luxury of venting a weak resentment on the universe. He observed that bad men were
more efficient in action than good men, and duly entered
the observation. He hoped for a time when the just cause
should have advocates as consistent and energetic as those
who serve the evil cause. He saw no reason why the just
cause should not have such support. For himself, he set
about a rehabilitation of Utopianism by disciplining himself in "more wise desires, simpler manners." He had a
moral realism which we must respect. Only those who are
debauched by sentimentalism find Wordsworth ethically
dull.

As the golden decade was drawing to its end Wordsworth wrote two odes, the *Ode to Duty* and the ode on the
Intimations of Immortality. Both fall between 1804 and
1806. To these should be added, perhaps, *The Happy
Warrior* (1805). The "Happy Warrior" is a person

> Who, doomed to go in company with Pain,
> And Fear, and Bloodshed, miserable train!
> Turns his necessity to glorious gain;
> In face of these doth exercise a power
> Which is our human nature's highest dower;
> Controls them, and subdues, transmutes, bereaves,
> Of their bad influence, and their good receives;
>
> . . . .
>
> As tempted more, more able to endure,
> As more exposed to suffering and distress;
> Thence, also, more alive to tenderness.

The Fenwick Notes give a deceptive clue to the identity of the warrior; they mention Lord Nelson. Wordsworth's free hand, like the magician's, may have been
pointing in Nelson's direction; his other hand was busy
behind his back at the autobiographical tangle. Like
Stephen's essay, the poem was a lay sermon which Wordsworth preached to himself on the text, "Waste not." No
schoolboy, set to learn and recite the lines, can possibly

understand them. Only a grown man can begin to grasp
them. Meanwhile, the happiness of the hero of the poem
is a temper which is deliberately willed, and the lines, salutary though they may be, are not convincing. We are
made more resolute by reading these verses, we cannot say
that they radiate a contagious happiness.

Precisely the opposite is true of the poem on immortality. Although it is a dirge sung at the passing of the
muse, it is, none the less, a joyful affirmation. Wordsworth
believed that it was better to have been a poet and to have
lost the glory of the calling, than never to have been a poet
at all. He celebrates the esthetic experience as being its own
warrant and its own reward. To the last our embers keep
something of its glory. Therefore the final note of regret
in the ode on the *Intimations of Immortality* should not
overpower the tones of joy which it remembers and reaffirms. Since that joy was a religious experience Wordsworth, with all the mystics, was beyond good and evil
whenever his world was bathed in its celestial light.
Morality, with its doctrine of duty, takes us over only
when inspiration fails us. Wordsworth's religion and his
ethics do not coincide. They deal with life at distinct
times, each having its own season. In particular, duty assumes the direction of life when inspiration has departed.

Wordsworth's moral reflections have a certain aridity,
but the moralizings of all mystics have been arid in like
manner. The life of the mystic is divided between short
periods of illumination, with a consequent relaxation of
moral strain, and long periods of uncertainty with the
ethical vigilance required by that state of soul. The moral
regimen of mysticism is intended to deal only with periods
when certainty is withheld, and therefore it reflects the
sense of insecurity and of dryness which marks the uninspired stretches of life. At such times we can only do our
duty.

Wordsworth reconciled himself to the loss of inspiration

because he believed that inspiration came to maturity as an understanding of life. He made an armistice, if not a peace, with "the years that bring the philosophic mind." The ephemeral sensations and fugitive emotions which are used in the making of a poem seem in retrospect to have been the heat by means of which agnosticism is fashioned into faith. In age we know what man and nature and human life are. Poetry is thus the means to a philosophic end. I doubt whether this is a sound theory of esthetics, or whether Wordsworth would have invoked it when his powers were at their height. The experience of the artist must be an end in itself, a direct address and access to reality requiring no supplement. To make poetry a means to some end other than itself, even so high an end as philosophy, is to vitiate it. Wordsworth fails when he labors the greater worth of the years that bring the philosophic mind. He does not convince us because he never convinced himself. If there be any ground for Matthew Arnold's distrust of the philosophical element in Wordsworth's work, we find it in the studied assertion that poetry is merely a precursor of philosophy. There is a calm serenity over the closing stanzas of the ode on the *Intimations of Immortality*, in which the rewards of the reflective life are celebrated. But the stanzas are not satisfactory; their calm, if not deliberately willed, seems an affectation. At the best they suggest the leaden serenity of a late November afternoon.

Let us not do Wordsworth an injustice. He was a mystic, and therefore liable to his meed of that *accidie* which mysticism promises its exemplars. Had he claimed an inspiration which was constant and permanent we should know that he was a pretender. Therefore he is under bond to intimate that we are unprofitable servants when we have done that which it is our duty to do. In morality there is wanting the margin which makes religion, or poetic inspiration, what it is.

Two quite independent strands have been twisted together to make up Wordsworth's ethics: the appeal to an alchemy whereby all our pain may be turned to joy, the appeal to duty when inspiration is in default. Each is valid, in its own terms, but the two are quite distinct and should not be identified. The former is an attempt to solve the problem of evil, the latter is an attempt to define the relation of religion and morality.

CHAPTER XIII

Retrospect

THE early years gave the Wordsworth household few creature comforts.

At Dove Cottage the work of the household had been doubled by overcrowding; now at Allan Bank it was doubled by the smoky chimneys. The smoke was enough to break the heart of any house-keeper. No sooner were the dishes washed after a meal and set up in the pantry than they were covered with smoke, and unfit to be used when the next meal-time came round; the chairs and newly contrived carpets and the fresh-sewn curtains became filthy. . . . There were days when Mary and William sat working in William's study, all involved in smoke, and working with streaming eyes. . . . On one day of high wind they could have no fire in the house except in William's study, and they had to do the cooking there, until at last that room was thick as if with fog and there was nothing for it but to retire to bed.[1]

The move from Allan Bank to the parsonage did not improve matters. The smoke was better, but the mud was worse.

The house stood in the middle of a field which could not be drained, and which the wet weather had turned into a mire, so that the children coming in and out constantly brought more mud indoors. The workmen, who were still busy with the repairs, seemed to take a malevolent pleasure in treading mud and lime into all the floors. It looked as if the workmen would be in the house most of the summer, for they were at work on the

---

1. Catherine MacDonald MacLean, *Dorothy Wordsworth, the Early Years* (London: Chatto and Windus, 1932), pp. 295–296.

kitchen chimney; and on the putting of new chimney pieces into all the rooms.[1]

Poets are not guaranteed immunity to life's little annoyances, but Wordsworth's share of them seems to have been in excess. Dorothy tells us that for years he had no study of his own and worked in a crowded sitting-room, where all the noises of the kitchen could be heard, and where the children played about his feet. Until the friendship was broken, Coleridge was tacitly accepted as a member-at-will of the Wordsworth household. Hartley and Derwent were usually with him and in his absence often came alone. When she was certain of not meeting her husband, Mrs. Coleridge was apt to appear, and to stay as suited her convenience. Sara Hutchinson became one of the family, and the other Hutchinsons were frequent visitors. De Quincey was added to the intimate circle and was constantly in and out. As the poet's fame spread, callers multiplied, and toward the end, when the Lake District had been discovered and Rydal Mount had become a pilgrim shrine, the family had to flee their home in the summer time to keep some shreds of decent privacy. The whole impression is that of a man denied the solitude which was the first condition for the exercise of his genius.

As we re-read the sources it sometimes seems as if the answer to Wordsworth's decline were staring us in the face, in these terms, and that we need manufacture no sophisticated account of other causes. Most of the best work had been finished before the children began to arrive. Thereafter the "dreary intercourse of daily life" crowded out the muse. Despite the poet's statement that this intercourse did not disturb him, the words suggest a mounting grievance and the awareness of a task perpetually deferred. If it was not the smoke or the mud, it was something else which, after about 1803–04, was always getting between

1. *Ibid.*, p. 349.

Wordsworth and his work. Being William Wordsworth, he could not let the chimneys smoke and the mud accumulate. Even if he had been above such creaturely distractions, he had much too proper a feeling for his wife and sister to delegate the difficulties to them. Happily for him he was the sort of man whose conscience approved attention to domestic details. He took a fussy pleasure in overseeing the repair jobs. He could not believe that these tasks could be rightly planned and well done without his supervision. The masons around Grasmere grudgingly admitted that Wordsworth knew something about chimneys, but they must have found him a nuisance.

For years there were money troubles. The Wordsworth household was never in actual poverty, but not until the 1830's had it worked well to windward of chronic anxiety. Wordsworth had a circle of would-be patrons, in particular Lord Lonsdale, who were ready to help him; but he was far too much of a freeman to fall back upon others. From time to time he accepted gifts from his friends; but, unlike Coleridge, he was unable to delegate to the generous friend nearest at hand the support of himself and his family. Occasional bequests helped matters. His poetic start in life had been made possible by the money he had received from Raisley Calvert. His wife had kinsmen who were, as the times went, rich, and now and then one of them left her something. But none of the adventitious money warranted Wordsworth in relaxing his own efforts.

Then there were the genuine tragedies. The death of his brother John, lost with the *Abergavenny* on the Shambles of the Bill of Portland in 1805, numbed Wordsworth for many months. Dorothy piteously describes him as sunk in apathy. The connection of the event with the subtle change coming over his poetic powers at that time has never been sufficiently examined. Perhaps it cannot be, since Wordsworth hid his after-thoughts in silence. Frequent and serious illness of the children followed, sadly concluded seven or eight years later with the deaths, first, of Catherine and then of Tom.

It is quite clear, therefore, that at the time when Wordsworth's poetic powers were being impaired by other causes, these incidents and accidents of private life must have hastened rather than retarded the decline. Yet we may not conclude that of themselves they caused his decline. The poet's anxieties and sorrows were simply stages in a progressive identification with the common heart of man, and he was much too consistent a person to shirk in his own life troubles which he had celebrated in the lives of others. Saint Augustine, speaking of the theater, asks in his *Confessions*, "Why is it that man likes to taste an unnecessary sorrow, by beholding distressing and tragical events which he would not wish to happen to himself?" Wordsworth was entirely wanting in any such theatricality. He had little or no interest in making copy of his private difficulties for the sake of getting literary effects. There is autobiography in Wordsworth's verse, but there is no exhibitionism. His feelings were instinctively direct and clean, leaving no room for dramatic self-pity.

Thus we cannot say of him that he was "a nerve o'er which do creep the else unfelt oppressions of the earth." Indeed it was an inability in maturity to exploit his own troubles in verse which kept him out of the society of lesser poets and still isolates him as a problematical character. On the other hand he was not, initially, an insensitive man. From all accounts he had been aggressively ardent, even passionate, in his youth. Conversely when he recoiled into pure passivity, he was delicately attuned to so much of the world as spoke to him. His delineation of the poet, whether as creator or receiver, is self-description.

How then are we to account for that strong suggestion of something very like to callousness which is given by the story of the later years? The man, in mid-life and in age, was too much insulated. His nerves, so far from being

naked to the world, were encased in a non-conductor. I
can only conclude that his apparent insensitiveness was a
protective device, developed more or less instinctively, to
defend a genuine sensitiveness of mind and heart against
both the hostility of the wider world and the private sorrows and distractions of the more intimate world. The
result was a mode of living with others which fell much too
near unvarnished selfishness.

Read Crabb Robinson's letters to the Wordsworths.
The good Robinson wrote to Dorothy and Mary far more
often than to William. His constant references to the
poet's professed distaste for personal talk suggest a reluctance to break the silence imposed upon family and friends
alike. Meanwhile he was the London errand-boy for the
Grasmere household. He went shopping for the candles
and the soap, he delivered manuscripts, forwarded proofs,
bought books, made endless inquiries as to the relative
merits of various investments. He was liaison officer between Grasmere and Paris. Altogether his commissions
for Wordsworth must have been no small part of the du-
ties, if not the mercies, of each returning day.

He put himself at the poet's disposal as a traveling com-
panion and got small thanks for his pains. Wordsworth
cannot have concealed from his friend the disapproval
which he did not hesitate to vent in letters home:

> There are so many things in habit and inclination in which
> Mr. R and I differ. . . . He takes delight in loitering about
> towns, gossiping; attending reading rooms, and going to coffee
> houses; and at *table d'hotes*, etc., gabbling German or any other
> tongue, all which things and practices are my abomination. . . .
> In this and a hundred other things, our tastes and habits are
> quite at variance, though nobody can be more obliging in giving
> up his own; but you must be aware that it is very unpleasant for
> me to require it.[1]

---

1. W. W. to M. W.

Not only so, but Crabb Robinson's Rydal friends twitted him about his Unitarianism. The words are the words of Mary, but the spirit is that of William:

The restraint I feel is sometimes unpleasant. And now & then I break out. Telling an anecdote the other day of signing myself at a German inn which required to know my religion — Muggletonian — Mrs. W said You might have signed it *Muddle*tonian.[1]

Wordsworth's humor was always clumsy, and often so clumsy as to hurt. If Robinson felt no shame or pain, we who would be with him apologists for the poet cannot read the letters without feeling a vicarious pain and shame.

So of the poet's correspondence with Henry Reed;[2] it were better for Wordsworth's reputation that it had never been published. It is, on the poet's part, a sorry display of an overbearing attitude and a want of common human courtesy which confirms the impression we get from his letters to Crabb Robinson. Henry Reed, a professor of English in the University of Pennsylvania, brought out in 1837 the first American edition of Wordsworth's poems, and was for many years thereafter the poet's ablest advocate in the United States. Wordsworth did not like America and made little effort to conceal his dislike. Reed, nothing daunted, was a devotee and missionary for the cause in a dark continent. He might have been allowed, in the protracted correspondence, decent recognition and gratitude. But, no. The letters are mainly concerned with the fluctuations of the American stock market, and Reed was treated as an unpaid financial adviser. He must bear the entire burden of disgrace incurred by the State of Pennsylvania when it repudiated in 1842 certain bonds in which the Grasmere circle, Miss Fenwick in particular, had

1. H. C. R. to T. R.
2. Leslie N. Broughton, *Wordsworth and Reed* (Ithaca: Cornell University Press, 1933).

invested. The patient Reed is sharply rapped over the knuckles:

> For my own part, I cannot but hope, that notwithstanding the evil example of other States, & the bad, or rather no principles of the dregs of your democracy, all will yet come round. . . . As to Mississippi & some other States, I think they are abandoned to utter profligacy & in the course of a righteous Providence will be doomed to suffer for their iniquity.[1]

> I must own that I cannot but blush for the state of Pennsylvania, and my hopes of justice sink in spite of all that you have, though with much caution and delicacy, said to keep them up.[2]

Professor Reed's letters in reply, which naturally would have discussed poetry and with the slightest encouragement would have burst into profuse blossom of praise, were forced to become running comments on American stocks and bonds. He cannot resist from time to time a hungry request for some word on literary matters from the oracle. There are shy, tentative appeals for a response in kind. But these are ignored and languish in neglect. The bulk of the correspondence had to be confined to money matters.

> There is not much to be hoped from the present Legislature! . . . Mis F's $35000 — sold at 39 would give $13650, which invested in R.R. Loans at 65 — would give $21000 (par value) which bearing interest as they do at 6% per cent would yield $1260 instead of $1750 which she used to receive on her State Loans. . . .[3]

> The last annual report of the Directors of the Philad. Wilmington and Baltimore R.R.Co. (January 1843) should be examined. . . . The whole funded debt of the Company is not quite Three Million Dollars. ($2,972,887 — 16/100): the interest on which at 6 per Cent is about $180,000. The receipts last year were very nearly 470,000: the expenses of the road were nearly 240,000. . . .[3]

---

1. W. W. to H. R., March 1, 1842.
2. W. W. to H. R., September 4, 1842.
3. H. R. to W. W., March 15, 1843.

Dorothy came too near the truth when she said that William was "prudent." Yet would Wordsworth's glory have been greater had he condemned his wife and children during the productive years to grinding poverty and left them after his death to find shelter in "the House, misnamed of INDUSTRY"? He furnishes, indeed, a welcome respite from the usual story of the artist whose family is the vicarious victim of his want of prudence. No known theory of art puts Wordsworth out of bounds because he waived the chance of a rise in the principal of the "french threes" and is "inclined to prefer the English 4's."

What offends us is the excess of illiberality in Wordsworth's relation to his friends, — illiberality in Aristotle's meaning of that term, — the fact that he seems to have used them rather than to have enjoyed them. The sources indicate a man who treated his friends as means to his own ends rather than as ends in themselves. It is here that something very like self-centeredness appears the dominant quality in the man. Do what I will, I cannot escape the suggestion. It obtrudes itself in the personal story over all the last forty years, revealing either a nature or a character from which I recoil. I am not attracted to the grown man.

The illiberality may be merely "the light of common day" falling on a figure from which the glory has departed. And yet I suspect that in those embers there lived something of the poet even at his best. For great artists have no alternative but to take themselves seriously. If they believe themselves to be the instruments for inspiration, they owe the instrument decent respect and care. The artist is in a difficult position. He must obtrude and assert himself. If he is an authentic genius, he must sooner or later take toll of the world's recognition. In the field of art as in the field of religion he must, in the meantime, make his forehead like flint as he faces the still unconverted world. Any show of weakness is rightly interpreted as want of faith in his own powers. You cannot judge him by the canons which you apply to men who have only talent, much less to the rank and file who are neither poets nor prophets. Yet the world will always construe the artist's necessary self-regard as selfishness and pride.

Now the premise for any appraisal of Wordsworth's character is the conviction, which dawned early and lasted to the end, that he was a dedicated poet. In Wordsworth this conviction came to a man who was already self-reliant by nature. It was not as though the poetic afflatus had been vouchsafed to an initially self-distrustful person. He was no Cowper or Francis Thompson. Wordsworth would have been a difficult man to get along with if he had never been a poet, because of a native stubbornness and want of pliability. He lacked, as his freeman type always lacks, any approach to finesse in life's give and take. There was from the first a heritage of bluntness and a square-toed address to life.

You have, thus, in Wordsworth the poet's assurance of his high calling superimposed upon a nature already over-endowed with self-reliance. The consequent intensification of nature by art gives to the contours of Wordsworth's character the lines which irritated so many of his contemporaries, and which sadden us. We could wish that he had been a more open-hearted man. Yet, unless we are to hold him personally chargeable for the defects of his north-country type, and unless we are to make him the scape-goat for the entire burden of necessary self-regard among inspired men, we must temper our ungenerous judgment.

The bleakness of Wordsworth's character has its sources in a quality which we may describe as impersonality. Once off the safe ground of the best poems you never feel that you are getting at the real man. You know that from 1797 to 1806 there was a real man there; you wonder whether behind the protective self-concern of the later years that man is still alive. You are impatient to get through the forbidding exterior, if only to satisfy yourself once for all that the soul of the artist is either living or dead. Meanwhile you do not feel that the friends of his later years ever came fully alive for him. The poet is always keeping them at arm's length. He sees them as trees walking in his scene, as things which may be used for his own ends. He does not see other human beings for what they are in themselves. That is your mounting grievance against the William Wordsworth whom you have tried to know, and to whom you still owe a debt of gratitude which he seems to forbid your paying in person.

Now this chill impersonality, so patent in the uninspired years, is surely nothing but the perpetuation of a temper which had been essential to the inspired years. For all great art is touched by a strange impersonality. Only thus can it achieve universality. In his best poetry Wordsworth rises to a truth and beauty which are beyond the varieties of individualism. The supra-individual quality is what we mean by impersonality; something so elemental and so vast that it transcends the diversities of human nature. All of Wordsworth's subjects are, in his most austere work, treated in this impersonal way. Michael is not a mere category or type. He was not arrived at by a generalization made after much sampling the shepherds of the district. He was, as a matter of fact, suggested in the first instance by a single individual. But in his finished state the Michael of the poem has achieved, at Wordsworth's hands, an impersonal quality like that of the scene with which he is identified. He compasses all sorts and conditions of men.

Wordsworth dealt with himself in the same way. He has a good deal to say of his poetic vocation and of his zeal in following it. He mentions more than once the strange duality in his self-consciousness. He was "two consciousnesses." There was the dedicated poet, and then there was the workaday householder and stamp-clerk. The man accepted the poet quite dispassionately, as one might accept a major fact in nature — a mountain or the open sea. The man went about his human business, knowing that at any moment he might be suddenly drafted and wholly absorbed by the poet. It was the business of the man to guard jealously the endowment of the poet, and to serve him without question when summoned. I can see no sign that the man was personally vain for the poet. The fact of the poet was of such dimensions that personal pride would have been presumptuous. It is true that the poet lacked a sense of perspective and sometimes attached to his work a value which it lacked. But this was a flaw in the poet rather than a moral defect in the man.

To all this we have an illuminating parallel in the person of the religious mystic. The mystic manifests the same dispassionateness toward his spiritual experience, and takes a like objective interest in his experience of ecstasy. The ecstasy itself, however, is not something which he has achieved and of which therefore he may be personally proud. It is a transcendent mystery vouchsafed him by divine grace. Hence a daily levitical business goes on in the courts outside the sanctuary where the saintly self keeps vigil, and in the outer court we find a thoroughly matter-of-fact attitude toward the Holy of Holies which stands in its own right and at another level of life. The secret of Wordsworth's character seems to me to lie somewhere in this area.

Mary and Dorothy and Crabb Robinson — and even Henry Reed across the sea — must have realized that Wordsworth was still more impersonal in his dealing with himself than in his dealings with them. Therefore they were able to endure what otherwise would have been his intolerable detachment. If they were slaves of the poet, so also was the man Wordsworth. If the poet was hard on them, he was still harder on the earthen vessel which was himself. Precisely because Wordsworth was, in this matter, consistent we learn finally to tolerate, though not without sympathy for its victims, that insensibility toward others which was a corollary of his impersonal attitude toward his vocation. His apparent defects of character in later life are the afterglow of what had once been a necessary condition for his art. We could wish that the twilight had not been so prolonged. A swift tropical night, coming after a shorter day, might have been kinder to his reputation. But, as it is, we have a dogged consistency which was both Wordsworth's making and his unmaking. Without that stubborn strain he might conceivably have been reborn at the end of the golden decade as a poet after quite another kind. With it, his life both as a man and as a poet had to run a straight course to its end. If his own family and friends bore with him because, in these matters, he was harder on himself than on them, we can do no less. It is a mistake to try to extenuate him, making him in maturity a more lovable man than he was. We had best leave the hard lines as we see them, realizing that only by so doing shall we be able to understand the strange energy of the great years.

Possibly Wordsworth realized his defects better than we can. His self-knowledge was more acute than is commonly supposed. If this be so, then we may have here the ground for his insistence that a poet's life is immaterial to an understanding of his verse, and should be left untold and unstudied. It has been the misfortune of Wordsworth the poet that in recent years he has been too much supplanted by Wordsworth the man. Aside from the French adventures there is little in his life that pays the printing or repays the reading. The man lived, for his last forty or fifty years, a relatively uninteresting life. The smoking chimneys at Allan Bank and the respective merits of "french threes" and "English 4's" in the 1820's—to say nothing of the six per cent bonds of the Philadelphia, Wilmington, and Baltimore R. R. — do not bulk large on the horizon of the history of the nineteenth century. We thresh the straw solely in the hope that some kernel of significant fact may be discovered which will help us understand more clearly the nature of the great harvest. We search the personal record for clues to the impersonal genius.

Too much of the recent criticism of Wordsworth blames him for not being some other kind of poet or man. We are fretful that we cannot recast him in a different mould nearer to our liking. Because we cannot rise to his heights when he is at his best, we resent him and parody him. We need a new generosity toward him, a willingness to let him be himself.

I lay down my Wordsworth again, grateful to that discriminating and generous soul, Crabb Robinson, for having, once for all, set these matters in the right perspective; the passage comes in a letter to Landor:

He is after all W: In all cases I care little what a man is not — I look to what he is — And W has written a hundred poems, the least excell^t of wch I wo^d not sacrifice to give him that openness of heart y^o require — Productive power acts by means of concentration.